MW00452497

GREAT
EVENTS

in

AMERICAN
HISTORY

GREAT
EVENTS
in
AMERICAN
HISTORY

Rebecca Price Janney

GOD & COUNTRY™
PRESS

Great Events in American History

Copyright © 2009 by Rebecca Price Janney

Published by God and Country Press, an imprint of AMG Publishers
6815 Shallowford Rd.
Chattanooga, Tennessee 37421

All rights reserved. Except for brief quotations in printed reviews,
no part of this publication may be reproduced, stored in a retrieval system, or transmitted in any form or by any means (printed, written,
photocopied, visual electronic, audio, or otherwise) without the prior
permission of the publisher.

ISBN 13: 978-0-89957026-6
ISBN 10: 0-89957-026-7
First Printing—October 2009

Scripture quotations marked (NIV) are taken from the Holy Bible,
New International Version®, NIV®. Copyright © 1973, 1978, 1984 by
Biblica, Inc.™ Used by permission of Zondervan. All rights reserved
worldwide.

Scripture quotations marked (KJV) are taken from the Holy Bible,
King James (Authorized) Version, which is in the public domain.

Cover designed by Garborg Design Works, Savage, MN
Interior design and typesetting by Reider Publishing Services,
    West Hollywood, CA
Edited and Proofread by Dan Penwell and Rick Steele

Printed in the United States of America
15 14 13 12 11 10 09 –D– 7 6 5 4 3 2 1

For my son, David Harrison Janney.
I will cherish your birth date in my heart forever.

INTRODUCTION

1492
July 4, 1776
1812
December 7, 1941
June 6, 1944

THE SOUND of those dates inspired wonder in me when my teachers brought the events, people, and times they commemorated to life. I could just imagine hallowed places where brave men and women established a land of opportunity and freedom in an oppressed world. What happened long ago—the decision of the Founding Fathers to declare independence from Great Britain— echoes down the hallways of time to impact our lives today. The courage of American GI's in World War II to rescue civilization from tyranny when they stormed the beaches at

Normandy, France. The conviction of civil rights workers as they fought to overcome racial prejudice.

In *Great Dates in American History* I share faith-based stories related to each of these important occurrences. Some of the dates are specific days while others cover a span of months, or a certain year, but all of them demonstrate the myriad ways in which God has shed his grace on America. Knowing what happened on noteworthy dates helps us better understand how we became as we are today and assists us in learning from the past as we move toward the future. I use compelling stories that put events that seem merely secular at first glance into the context of God's activity. Rather than a dry recounting of historical facts and figures, this book provides a fascinating account of major dates from both a temporal and eternal perspective.

May these inspire, challenge, and encourage your own spirit as you live in such a time as this.

Rebecca Price Janney

Great Events in American History

October 12, 1492 In Fourteen Hundred and
Ninety-two Columbus Sailed the Ocean Blue   1

April 29, 1607 The Establishment of the First
Permanent English Colony in North America   5

Autumn 1620 The Mayflower Arrives in America   9

1754–1763 The French and Indian War   13

The 1760s and 1770s Events Leading to War   17

July 4, 1776 The Declaration of Independence   2

October 19, 1781 The British Surrender
at Yorktown   23

September 17, 1787 The Signing of the United
States Constitution   27

1803 The Louisiana Purchase   31

The War of 1812   35

1836 Remember the Alamo   39

1861–1865 The War Between the States   43

January 1, 1863 The Emancipation Proclamation   47

April 9, 1865 Surrender at Appomattox   51

April 14, 1865 The Assassination of
Abraham Lincoln   55

1898 The Spanish-American War   59

September 5, 1901 President McKinley's
Assassination   63

December 17, 1903 The Wright Brothers'
First Successul Flight   67

April 18, 1906 The San Francisco Earthquake   71

April 1912 The Sinking of the *Titanic*   75

1914–1918 World War I:
"The War to End All Wars"   79

October 29, 1929 The Stock Market Crash   83

December 7, 1941 Pearl Harbor: "A Date
Which Will Live in Infamy"   87

June 6, 1944 D-Day   91

August 6, 1945 Hiroshima: The First Atomic
Bomb Is Dropped   95

1954 Supreme Court Decision: Brown v.
Board of Education of Topeka, Kansas   99

December 1955 Civil Rights Movement:
Rosa Parks Refuses to Give Up Her Seat   103
on a Public Bus

October 4, 1957 *Sputnik* Satellite Is Launched   107

October 1962 The Cuban Missile Crisis   111

November 22, 1963 The Assassination of   115
John F. Kennedy

January 1968 The Tet Offensive   119

April 4, 1968 and June 5, 1968
The Assassinationsof Martin Luther King, Jr.   123
and Robert F. Kennedy

July 20, 1969 The First Man Walks on the Moon   129

May 1970 The Shootings at Kent State University   133

1972 Détente: President Nixon in Russia
and China   137

August 9, 1974 Richard Nixon Resigns
as President   141

November 4, 1979–January 20, 1981
The Iranian Hostage Crisis   145

January 28, 1986 The *Challenger* Disaster   149

1989 The Fall of Soviet Communism   153

August 2, 1990–February 28, 1991 The Persian
Gulf War   161

April 19, 1995 The Oklahoma City Bombing   165

September 11, 2001 The Terrorist Attacks
on America   169

Acknowledgments   177

OCTOBER 12, 1492

In fourteen hundred and ninety-two Columbus sailed the ocean blue.

WHEN EUROPE emerged from the Middle Ages at the end of the fifteenth century, various countries on that continent set out to explore new lands. Stories of exotic places reached the emerging middle classes from those who had traveled to Asia and the Middle East. The lure of spices and precious metals stirred the hearts of some Europeans, who began to dream of finding a northwest passage to the Orient to secure glory and riches for themselves and the nations that sponsored them. Others longed to introduce the Lord Jesus to those who had never heard of him. They set out to fulfill his "great commission" from Matthew 28:19 (NIV) to "go and make disciples of all nations, baptizing them in the name of the Father and of the Son and of the Holy Spirit . . . ."

Rivalries intensified among Europe's seafaring nations with Portugal dominating the other western powers at the start of what historians call the Modern Age. Spain, Holland, England, and Italy all nipped at its heels, however, and in the end, it was an Italian explorer sailing under the Spanish flag who changed world history.

Christopher Columbus was born in 1451 in Genoa, Italy to a middle class family. By the age of ten, he was beginning to taste the life of a mariner, gaining various commissions and jobs that led to his eventually marrying the daughter of a Portuguese nobleman. His dream was to find a western route to the "Indies," and he appealed to the Portuguese king to fund his voyage, but King John II turned him down twice. He also sought favor from England's Henry VII, but by the time that monarch got around to answering the request, King Ferdinand and Queen Isabella of Portugal had commissioned Columbus to find the New World for Spain.

Under their authority, Columbus initiated exploration of the Americas, sailing with three ships, the *Nina*, the *Pinta*, and the *Santa Maria*. Five weeks after leaving on the historic voyage, Rodrigo de Triana on the *Pinta* spotted land (the Bahamas) hours before dawn on October 12, 1492. Around noon Columbus planted a Spanish banner on the beach and told his men to kneel as he named the land "San Salvador" after Jesus. Then he prayed:

O Lord, Almighty and everlasting God, by Thy holy Word Thou hast created the heaven, and the earth, and the sea; blessed and glorified be Thy Name, and praised be Thy Majesty, which hath deigned to use us, Thy humble servants, that Thy holy Name may be proclaimed in this second part of the earth.[1]

Although Columbus claimed the land for Spain, he actually answered to a higher authority. According to an obscure book written in his hand, Columbus ventured out into the unknown not just for spices, nor gold, nor silver, and not for his own glory or even Spanish domination of the seas, but to win the hearts of the natives for Christ.[2] He wrote:

> It was the Lord who put into my mind (I could feel His hand upon me) the fact that it would be possible to sail from here to the Indies. All who heard of my prospect rejected it with laughter, ridiculing me. There is no question that the inspiration was from the Holy Scriptures.[3]

In addition, Columbus insisted that maps and mathematical skills were less important in guiding him than were the Scriptures that he believed foretold the momentous journey. He saw himself undertaking the dangerous voyage for the sake of Christ's Kingdom above all.

END NOTES

1. Rebecca Price Janney, *Great Stories in American History*. (Camp Hill, PA: Horizon Books, 1998), 5–7.
2. Ibid.
3. Ibid.

April 29, 1607

The Establishment of the First Permanent English
Colony in North America—Jamestown

I T TOOK MORE than four grueling months for the men and boys of the Virginia Expedition to cross the Atlantic Ocean in their quest to establish North America's first permanent English settlement. Others had gone before, including the failed Roanoke Island colony of the late 1580s. This latest venture endured intense storms that battered the three ships, so fragile by today's standards. On board the *Susan Constant,* Captain Christopher Newport commanded the voyage, accompanied by the Rev. Robert Hunt, the official chaplain.

A thirty-something Anglican vicar, Hunt had left his wife and two children in England to answer God's call to spread the gospel to people who had never heard of Jesus. Hunt suffered from acute seasickness on the voyage, as well as rumors from some of the superstitious crew who blamed the storms on his presence. The priest bore his infirmities with dignity and grace, and it was to him that Captain Newport often looked for wisdom and guidance as he navigated the turbulence both on his ships and on the open sea.

At last the three vessels arrived at the mouth of the Chesapeake Bay. Led by Hunt, the men erected a seven-foot oak cross on what they named "Cape Henry," in honor of the Prince of Wales. The men knelt on the beach while Hunt conducted a time of prayer in which he thanked God for bringing them safely across the ocean to "Virginia." (The earlier colonists had named the land for the Virgin Queen, Elizabeth I). He declared, ". . . from these very shores the Gospel shall go forth to not only this New World, but the entire world."[1]

Along with thanks and praise, he spoke the words of caution that the British Royal Council had uttered from the Bible regarding their expedition that, "Every plantation, which my Heavenly Father hath not planted, shall be rooted up." Then Hunt raised his hands upward and declared that the new land would be not only for England and King James, but for the glory of Almighty God.

Robert Hunt lived just a year longer until he succumbed to one of the diseases that ravaged Jamestown. In that short time, however, he made a lasting impression. He held prayer and regular services under an old sail while the first English church in North American was being built. He helped settle many disputes and factions among the colonists and guided them through the initial, brutal time of "seasoning" as they adjusted to the whims and wiles of their new land and each other. Of him it was said, "It is impossible to rate too highly the character and work of the aforesaid Robert Hunt, Chaplain of the Colony."[2]

For example, in January 1608 a fire broke out, destroying much of the fort, including the entire contents of Hunt's library and all of his possessions. One of the other colonists recorded, however, that while "Good master Hunt lost all his library, and all that he had but the clothes on his back, yet none ever did see him repine at his loss . . . Yet we had daily Common Prayer morning and evening, every Sunday two sermons and every three months the Holy Communion till our Minister died."[3]

END NOTES

1. "Cape Henry: Spiritual Roots of a Nation" by Craig von Buseck, http://www.cbn.com/spirituallife/churchandministry/churchhistory/vonBuseck_CapeHenry_SpriritualRoots.aspx

2. "The Reverend Robert Hunt: The First Chaplain at Jamestown," National Park Service , U.S. Department of the Interior," http://www.nps.gov/jame/historyculture/the-reverend-robert-hunt-the-first-chaplain-at-jamestown.htm

3. Ibid.

Autumn, 1620

The Mayflower Arrives in America

I N THE EARLY part of the seventeenth century, England was a brutal place. According to one source, it had become "a nation without a soul." A beggar could die of exposure in a merchant's doorway, and the merchant, arriving to open up in the morning would be irate at having to step over the body. . . ."[1]

There was turmoil within England's official, Anglican Church, and two groups within its fold desired to bring about a deeper and higher spirituality. The Puritans hoped to reform the church internally while the Pilgrims believed the only lasting change could come from separating from it. In the fall of 1620 a little over one hundred men, women, and children from the Pilgrim community sailed for America in *The Mayflower* to pursue religious liberty and to better themselves in a land quite apart from Old England.

They chose a bad time to leave. It took them over two months to cross the ocean, and when they arrived at Cape Cod on November 9, it was far too late in the year to plant crops. More than half of the colonists died from illness as they tried to survive that first harsh winter in primitive dwellings without enough food. Of their plight, Governor William Bradford wrote:

> If they looked behind them, there was the mighty ocean which they had passed and was now as a main bar and gulf to separate them from all the civil parts of the world . . . What could now sustain them but the Spirit of God and His grace? May not and ought not the children of these fathers rightly say, "Our fathers were Englishmen which came over this great ocean, and were ready to perish in this wilderness; but they cried unto the Lord, and He heard their voice and looked on their adversity . . . [2]

In addition to the stark climate, the Pilgrims found difficulty in taming the wilderness of Massachusetts because they were mainly shopkeepers and people who had inhabited towns all their lives. They had incredible fortitude, however, convinced that they were in God's place in God's perfect timing. One of them remarked, "It is not with us as with other men, whom small things can discourage, or small discontentments cause to wish themselves at home again."[3]

Aided by a native American named Squanto, they learned how to plant corn and catch fish. Although times were hard, when *The Mayflower* returned to England for supplies the following April, no one decided to give up and go home—they *were* home.

In the fall as they observed their one-year anniversary in America, the Pilgrims celebrated the first Thanksgiving, a three-day feast that they shared with Chief Massasoit of the Wampanoag tribe and ninety of his people. Governor Bradford recorded, "Thus out of small beginnings greater things have been produced by His hand that made all things of nothing . . . and as one small candle may light a thousand; so the light here kindled hath shone unto many, yea, in some sort, to our whole nation."[4]

END NOTES

1. Rebecca Price Janney, *Great Stories in American History*. (Camp Hill, PA: Horizon Books, 1998), 14.
2. Ibid., 15–16.
3. Ibid., 16.
4. Ibid., 17.

1754–1763

The French and Indian War

IN 1755 the British General Edward Braddock marched on Fort Duquesne to seize control of it from the French. Before he reached the bastion in present-day Pittsburgh, the French routed his military and killed him. No longer were British settlements in western Pennsylvania, Maryland, or Virginia safe, nor were the Native Americans exclusively on the side of the British as in the past. Due to a series of military and political alliances in Europe, a full-scale war broke out that took in not only the American colonies, but reached as far as Europe and Asia, and all the way to the Philippines.

In America the conflict was known as the French and Indian War. When the Peace of Paris Treaty was signed in 1763 to end the hostilities, the victorious British had gained control of French Canada and Spanish-held Florida, as well as significant colonies in other parts of the world. "The British empire bestrode the world like a colossus; India gained, all North America to the Mississippi won, and the best of the West Indies; supremacy of the seas confirmed."[1]

During the conflict, one American-born British officer had a few close brushes with death, the first during the disastrous Braddock campaign. He had warned the general that he was walking into a situation quite unlike European combat, but the proud Braddock brushed him off. Every one of Braddock's officers, except that one, was either wounded or killed in the skirmish.[2] Of that young officer, the Rev. Samuel Davies said, "I cannot but hope that Providence has hitherto preserved in so signal a manner for some important service to his country."[3] In a letter to his brother back home to reassure him that reports of his death were premature, the officer acknowledged his indebtedness to God for his survival:

Dear Jack:

As I have heard since my arrival at this place, a cir-cumstantial acct. of my death and dying speech, I take this early opportunity of contradicting both, and of assuring you that I now exist and appear in the land of the living by the miraculous care of Providence, that protected me beyond all human expectation; I had 4 Bullets through my Coat, and two Horses shot under me, and yet escaped unhurt . . . I am Dear Jack, your most Affect. Brother.

George Washington [4]

END NOTES

1. Samuel Eliot Morison, Henry Steele Commager, and William E. Leuchtenburg, *The Growth of the American Republic, Volume One.* (New York: Oxford University Press, 1969), 120.

2. Peter A. Lillback, *George Washington's Sacred Fire.* (Bryn Mawr, PA: Providence Forum Press, 2006), 161.

3. Ibid., 162.

4. Ibid., 161–2.

The 1760s and 1770s

Events Leading to War

WHEN THE British won the French and Indian War, someone had to pay for the expense, and to that end, in 1765 the Crown imposed a Stamp Act, in which all legal documents were required to bear a British Stamp in order to be considered official. Naturally, the restriction irked the colonists but when the Townshend Acts of 1767 were put into place, they felt even angrier to be paying taxes on many everyday items imported from Britain, such as tea, paper, lead, glass, and paint. These were the beginnings of the birth pangs of rebellion as ill will further increased towards the mother country.

By 1770 many colonists, especially Bostonians, seethed with resentment, and on March 5, several people in that port city threw snowballs at British troops to demonstrate their antagonism. A riot ensued in which the British opened fire, killing four colonists—an event known as the Boston Massacre. When the British government announced that its East India Company would have a monopoly on tea sent to the colonies, the Sons of Liberty dressed as native Americans and boarded three ships in Boston Harbor. During that "tea party" on December 16, 1773, they dumped the despised beverage into the harbor.

Throughout May and June of 1774 the British imposed further restrictions aimed to quell the rebellion once and for all. Instead, the Coercive Acts, also known as the Intolerable Acts, solidified the Thirteen Colonies, and in September the first Continental Congress met in Philadelphia to discuss the worsening situation. Revolution was all but assured when on April 18, 1775, British General Thomas Gage was sent to Boston to enforce the Acts. At Lexington, he was met by armed colonists from "every Middlesex Village and farm."[1] The first battle of the American Revolution took place there, at Lexington and Concord, with "the shot heard round the world."[2]

Meanwhile, in the Virginia House of Burgesses, patriot Patrick Henry was giving his famous speech:

> There is no longer any room for hope. If we wish to be free . . . we must fight! I repeat it, sir, we must fight! An appeal to arms and to the God of hosts is all that is left us!
>
> They tell us, sir, that we are weak; unable to cope with so formidable an adversary. But when shall we

be stronger? Will it be the next week, or the next year? Will it be when we are totally disarmed, and when a British guard shall be stationed in every house? Shall we gather strength by irresolution and inaction? Shall we acquire the means of effectual resistance by lying supinely on our backs and hugging the delusive phantom of hope, until our enemies shall have bound us hand and foot? Sir, we are not weak if we make a proper use of those means which the God of nature hath placed in our power. The millions of people, armed in the holy cause of liberty, and in such a country as that which we possess, are invincible by any force which our enemy can send against us. Besides, sir, we shall not fight our battles alone. There is a just God who presides over the destinies of nations, and who will raise up friends to fight our battles for us. The battle, sir, is not to the strong alone; it is to the vigilant, the active, the brave.

. . .

Is life so dear, or peace so sweet, as to be purchased at the price of chains and slavery? Forbid it, Almighty God! I know not what course others may take; but as for me, give me liberty or give me death![3]

END NOTES

1. Henry Wadsworth Longfellow, "Paul Revere's Ride," Legal Language Services, http://www.legallanguage.com/poems/MidnightRide.html.

2. Ralph Waldo Emerson, "Concord Hymn," Wikipedia, *The Free Encyclopedia*, September 21, 2008, http://en.wikipedia.org/wiki/Concord_Hymn.

3. Patrick Henry, "Give Me Liberty or Give Me Death!" March 23, 1775, LibertyOnline, http://libertyonline.hypermall.com/henry-liberty.html.

6

July 4, 1776

The Declaration of Independence

ON MAY 10, 1775 the Second Continental Congress assembled in Philadelphia. Over the course of the next year, delegates moved steadily towards declaring independence from Great Britain. Edward Rutledge of South Carolina cautioned that the price of sovereignty would be painfully high and hoped that in spite of all that had taken place, the breach could still be healed. Benjamin Franklin told the gathering, "We must indeed all hang together, or most assuredly we will all hang separately."[1]

For three weeks, delegates traveled to the regions they represented to test public opinion. Was there adequate support for going to war against England? When they reconvened, they reviewed a draft of a declaration of independence, and John Adams of Massachusetts remarked, "Before God, I believe the hour has come. My judgement approves this measure, and my whole heart is in it. . . I am for the Declaration. It is my living sentiment, and by the blessing of God it shall be my dying sentiment. Independence now, and Independence forever!"[2]

In a mood of deep solemnity, the delegates took a vote, which ended in a 12–1 decision for independence. New York abstained. In the sweltering heat of the Pennsylvania State House—now Independence Hall—sunlight suddenly pierced the tall windows. A new nation had just been born, upholding its beginnings as a city upon a hill for the entire world to see. Breaking the reverent silence, John Hancock brought laughter to the delegates when he wryly commented, "Gentlemen, the price on my head has just been doubled!" After which, Sam Adams stood and declared, "We have this day restored the Sovereign, to Whom alone men ought to be obedient. He reigns in heaven and . . . from the rising to the setting sun, may His Kingdom come."[3]

END NOTES

1. Rebecca Price Janney, *Great Stories in American History.* (Camp Hill, PA: Horizon Books, 1998), 40.

2. Ibid., 41.

3. Ibid., 42.

October 19, 1781

The British Surrender at Yorktown

THE WAR that had begun at Lexington and Concord—with the "shot heard round the world" in the spring of 1775—ground to an end eight long years later in Yorktown, Virginia. George Washington and his fellow commanders had fashioned a scruffy army of sometimes determined, sometimes unwilling, often unpaid and underfed patriots and brought them to the brink of victory against the most effective army in the world.

At the urging of the Marquis de Lafayette, France sent 6,000 men under the command of General Jean-Baptiste Rochambeau to America's aid in 1780, followed by an impressive flotilla led by Admiral Francois Joseph Paul Grasse. The land force occupied Newport that summer, and a year later Grasse struck at British General Cornwallis's forces in the

Chesapeake. By September 30, 1781 the British were under siege.

Copying a scene from General Washington's play book in 1776, Cornwallis tried to secret his men across the York River, hoping that history would repeat itself. Back in late August 1776, the British had squeezed Washington's forces in Brooklyn. Badly outnumbered following the vicious slaughter of 1,500 men, the Americans decided not to face the formidable British again so soon. Washington would try instead to remove his army to Manhattan, an amazing feat in itself. He set out on the stormy night of August 28 while the British forces slept. When conditions cleared up around midnight, the troops ran the risk of being seen as well as heard by the British, but they continued. By dawn, Washington still needed at least three more hours to complete the evacuation. Just then, a thick fog rolled in. American Major Ben Tallmadge recalled, "it seemed to settle in a peculiar manner over both encampments. I recollect this peculiar providential occurrence perfectly well, and so very dense was the atmosphere that I could scarcely discern a man at six yards distance. . . ."[1] The fog lifted only after the last American had reached safety.

When, however, General Cornwallis tried this same tactic, it failed. Rather than have fog cover their movements, the British experienced such a violent storm and turbulent seas that their flight was frustrated.[2] On October 19 Cornwallis surrendered at Yorktown as military bands played, *The World Turned Upside Down*. The war was over. George Washington would conclude, "We have . . . abundant reason to thank Providence for its many favourable interpositions in our behalf. It has, at times been my only dependence for all other resources seemed to have fail'd (sic) us."[3]

END NOTES

1. Janney, 47.
2. Lillback, 575.
3. Ibid., 576.

September 17, 1787

The Signing of the United States Constitution

WHEN THE United States was born on July 4, 1776, a temporary government existed under the Articles of Confederation. By the end of the conflict, the new nation was struggling with war debt, and some states refused to shoulder their share of the burden— determined to promote their own interests at the expense of the new union. Those who had seen the thirteen former colonies through the perils of revolution gathered once again in Philadelphia, in May, 1787 to fix what was wrong with the existing government. It became clear that a new arrangement was in order. A great deal of animosity developed as arguments took place around issues such as representation. The more highly populated northern states, for example, argued that it should be based on population, but the more sparsely occupied southern states cried "unfair!"

At one point, it seemed that the union was about to break up because various sides were so deeply entrenched. At a critical moment, the elder statesman, Benjamin Franklin, addressed his fellow delegates:

In the beginning of the contest with Great Britain when we were more sensible of danger, we had daily prayers in this room for Divine protection. Our prayers, Sir, were heard, and they were graciously answered. All of us who were engaged in the struggle must have observed frequent instances of a superintending Providence in our favor ... And have we now forgotten this powerful Friend? Or do we imagine we no longer need His assistance?

I have lived, Sir, a long time, and the longer I live, the more convincing proofs I see of this truth: "that God governs in the affairs of man." And if a sparrow cannot fall to the ground without His notice, is it probable that an empire can rise without His aid?

We have been assured, Sir, in the Sacred Writings that except the Lord build the house, they labor in vain that build it. I firmly believe this. I also believe that without His concurring aid, we shall succeed in this political building no better than the builders of Babel; we shall be divided by our little, partial local interests; our projects will be confounded; and we ourselves shall become a reproach and a byword down to future ages. And what is worse, mankind may here-

after, from this unfortunate instance, despair of estab-
lishing government by human wisdom and leave it to
chance, war, or conquest.

I therefore beg leave to move that, henceforth,
prayers imploring the assistance of Heaven and its
blessing on our deliberation be held in this assembly
every morning before we proceed to business.[1]

On September 17, 1787 the new Constitution was
signed, a document that began, "We, the people of the United
States . . ." On that day as George Washington rose from a
chair that carried the design of a half-sun on the back,
Franklin observed, "I have often and often in the course of
this session . . . looked at that . . . without being able to tell
whether it was rising or setting; but now at length I have the
happiness to know that it is a rising and not a setting sun."[2]

END NOTES

1. Peter Marshall and David Manuel, *The Light and the Glory.*
(Grand Rapids, Baker Book House, 1977), 342–43.

2. Samuel Eliot Morison and Henry Steele Commager, *The
Growth of the American Republic, Volume Two.* (New York: Oxford
University Press, 1962), 250.

1803

The Louisiana Purchase

AT THE TURN of the eighteenth century, young America eagerly anticipated expanding into the vast territories to the West and enlarging the nation's trade network along the Mississippi River down to the Port of New Orleans. Both the Spanish and French had controlled the region known as Louisiana at different times, and France currently dreamed of reestablishing total sovereignty there under the Emperor Napoleon.

A twelve-year revolt of free blacks and slaves in the French colony of Saint-Domingue resulted in a victory for the insurgents. With French forces unable to re-establish control over that Caribbean colony, they were in no position to protect an American empire. Thus, the French were willing to sell Louisiana for a total of fifteen million dollars to the United

States. This vast area stretched from the southernmost parts of the U.S. upwards into two Canadian provinces.

In the decade before this acquisition, fully 94 percent of Americans resided in the east in the original Thirteen Colonies. Within fifty years of the signing of the Louisiana Purchase, however, only half of the country lived in the initial states.[1]

While the new territories attracted people who were hungry to attain land, as well as lawless individuals who wanted to live in their own proscribed way, many ministers of the gospel followed them into the frontier, preaching to them, as well as to native Americans that what life was really all about was Jesus Christ. It was what the Pilgrims and other early colonists, along with many during the Revolution, had lived and died for. It was what the Rev. James McGready brought to the people of remote Kentucky that resulted in a tremendous outpouring of the Holy Spirit, helping ignite the country's Second Great Awakening. Upon observing the revival firsthand, one visiting minister observed:

> There, on the edge of a prairie in Logan County, Kentucky, the multitudes came together and continued a number of days and nights encamped on the ground, during which time the worship was carried on in some part of the encampment. The scene was new to me and passing strange. It baffled description. Many, very many, fell down as men slain in battle, and continued for hours together in an apparently breathless and

motionless state, sometimes for a few minutes reviving and exhibiting symptoms of life by a deep groan or a piercing shriek, or by a prayer for mercy fervently uttered. After lying there for hours, they obtained deliverance. The gloomy cloud that had covered their faces seemed gradually and visibly to disappear, and hope in smiles brightened into joy. They would rise, shouting deliverance, and then would address the surrounding multitude in language truly eloquent and impressive. With astonishment did I hear men, women, and children declaring the wonderful works of God, and the glorious mysteries of the Gospel.[2]

END NOTES

1. Martin Marty, *Righteous Empire: The Protestant Experience in America*. (New York: Harper Torchbooks, 1970), 47.
2. Marshall and Manuel, 63.

The War of 1812

THE WINTER OF 1811–12 was the bitterest one in Great Britain since the plague of 1665. In addition, Napoleon closed virtually all of Western Europe to British goods, leaving the English in need of recovering its American market. The former colonies, however, were in no mood for conciliation, not after the British Navy had been continually impressing unwilling American seamen into their service and repeatedly violating U.S. territorial waters. Under President James Madison, the U.S. Congress declared war on Great Britain on June 18, 1812. Many Americans believed that if they did not go to war, the nation would once again became a British colony.

One of the most memorable events of that confrontation occurred on August 24, 1814. After the British overpowered American forces at Bladensburg, Maryland, they muscled their way into the new capital city, Washington. As troops burned most of the public buildings, including the White

House and the unfinished Capitol, officers ate a dinner left by the fleeing First Couple, a raid that amused the British and infuriated Americans. A violent thunderstorm followed by a tornado squelched the destructive incursion on the second day. As a result, the British started moving northward to sack Baltimore.

Along the way, they impressed a Methodist missionary into leading a service on the Sunday before their attack. Joshua Thomas thought of refusing them, but then he decided to exhort the men to faith in Christ since many of them would surely die in the battle. "I told them," he said, "that it was given to me by the Almighty that they could not take Baltimore, and would not succeed in their expedition."[1] Afterwards, many men thanked him for offering such a bold message, adding that they hoped he was wrong about the prophecy. Along the way to the mêlée, their fearless commanding officer Robert Ross boasted, "I'll eat in Baltimore tonight—or in hell."[2] Although the British threw everything they had at the Americans guarding Fort McHenry at the approach to the city, they did not prevail. And as Francis Scott Key wrote, the American flag "was still there" at the end of the impressive bombardment.

When the defeated British returned to their position at Tangier Island, Thomas Parson went out to meet them, asking if they had won. They dejectedly explained that many of their men had died in the futile attempt, including Major General Ross. One man said, "You seemed to be standing right before us, warning us against our attempt to take Baltimore."[3] Another said that his friend's last words were, "God bless Parson Thomas. He showed me the way to Christ, and now, though I die, I hope for mercy and salvation through the name of Jesus, and expect to meet that good man in heaven."[4] A different soldier admitted to Parson, "I never felt my sinfulness before God, until that Sunday you preached to us; and while the bullets were flying, and my comrades were falling on every hand . . . I cast myself on the merits of the Lamb of God, and now I feel at peace."[5]

On Christmas Eve of that year, the combatants signed the Treaty of Ghent in which America proved, once again, victorious and free.

END NOTES

1. Marshall and Manuel, 150.
2. Ibid., 151.
3. Ibid.". 155,
4. Ibid.
5. Ibid., 155–6.

1836

Remember the Alamo!

THE ALAMO in San Antonio, Texas is remembered for the famous battle that occurred there, one that eventually led to Texas's independence from Mexico. It all began after the Louisiana Purchase when Americans began to move westward into the wilds of the frontier to settle new homes and churches, schools, towns, and commercial centers. In 1821, Stephen Austin led a group of pioneers into Texas, then part of Mexico—a country that cast a wary eye on the men and women from America. They had good cause for their suspicion. While the Mexican government insisted that all immigrants to Texas be Roman Catholic, most of the Americans pouring in were Protestants.

It was also unlawful for them to hold slaves, but the Americans felt they needed such laborers for growing cotton and were unwilling to give them up. They technically freed their slaves and called them indentured servants, but it was still slavery. Two U.S. presidents tried to persuade Mexico to sell Texas, but the Mexicans refused all offers. They did, however, become alarmed when the settlers began to multiply like the Israelites had in Egypt, soon outnumbering the Mexicans.

In 1830 further settlement was forbidden, but the Mexican government failed to implement the ban. The American immigrants began to seek independence from Mexico, and by 1835 a rebellion had broken out. Led by the Mexican president, Santa Ana, his forces marched on San Antonio in February, 1836, leading 6,000 Mexicans against 187 Americans, who took refuge at the fortress Alamo. For ten days they held off the Mexicans, killing many of their soldiers, but when Santa Ana's men breached the walls and stormed inside, they slaughtered everyone, then unceremoniously burned the bodies. They marched on to yet another fort, Goliad, and continued their killing spree. Infuriated, the Texans declared independence on March 2 and followed Sam Houston, a charismatic politician and military figure, who led a victorious charge against the Mexicans crying, "Forward! Charge! Remember the Alamo! Remember Goliad!"[1] By the fall, Texas was on its way to becoming one of the United States.

Today, the Alamo is remembered as a valiant battle that resulted in poignant loss of life, and a confrontation that spurred those who remained to fight for their independence. It did not begin that way, however. In the early 1700s, the Spanish built many missions in East Texas in order to educate the natives who lived in the area after converting them to Christianity.

Originally called the Mission San Antonio de Valero, the Alamo, constructed of limestone and boasting a beautiful chapel, remained in use until 1793 when the mission went secular after all of the local population had been Christianized. From that time, it served a much different purpose—as a military compound. A company of Spanish soldiers took over the complex in 1803, and because they were from Alamo de Parras, inhabitants referred to them as the Alamo Company, and their new home as "The Alamo."[2]

END NOTES

1. John A. Garraty, Robert A. McCaughey, *The American Nation: A History of theUnited States.* (New York: Harper & Row, Publishers, 1987), 350.

2. "Alamo Mission in San Antonio," Wikipedia, *The Free Encyclopedia*, October 19, 2008, http://en.wikipedia.org/wiki/Alamo_Mission_in_San_Antonio

1861–1865

The War Between the States

ABRAHAM LINCOLN promised when he was
elected President in 1860 that he would recognize
slavery where it already existed in the South. In
spite of this assurance, however, those states immediately
began to secede from the Union with many believing that
Lincoln could not or would not keep his pledge. By that
time, the North and South had grown apart in many ways,
with slavery providing the biggest point of contention
between them.

The North had grown into a powerful industrial region
while the South maintained an agrarian economy and way of
life with slavery a crucial component. Its people resented any
intimation of the North's superior status, while the North
was a bastion of abolitionism against slavery. In the decade

prior to the Civil War, the states engaged in spirited debates about whether the territories being added in the west should be free or allow slavery.

By the time of Lincoln's inauguration in March 1861, Southern forces began to seize ports, customs houses, and post offices as they broke away from the Union. They also demanded that the federal officer in charge of Fort Sumter in South Carolina surrender to the Confederates, resulting in the first shots of the war. Most people on both sides believed that the conflict would be brief, but it took a total of four years and 620,000 lives lost with at least that many men wounded before it would conclude.

In both the North and the South, people of faith rushed to serve the afflicted. The United States Christian Commission organized to promote the spiritual and physical health of Union soldiers with the distribution of Bibles and religious literature, prayer and worship services, hospital work, financial and travel-related assistance, and the creation of kitchens that provided the right kind of food for men who had been wounded. Some 10,000 churches participated in that mission, collecting and dispersing $6 million.[1]

One USCC worker in Virginia came upon an especially dismal site on a hot July day where, on the second floor of a barn under the roof, sixty-five wounded soldiers barely endured the terrible heat. The volunteer distributed food, then asked the attending soldier if he would bathe the men's hands and feet. "I did not enlist to wash men's feet," the soldier shot back. "Bring me the water, then, and I will do it," said the Christian worker. It brought him joy to serve the Lord by washing all sixty-five of the soldiers' hands and feet.[2]

In the Confederate forces, many religious revivals broke out during the course of the war in which countless soldiers and officers were touched deeply by the Spirit of God. In the Army of Northern Virginia, General John B. Gordon had spent the winter of 1863–64 along the Rapidan River preparing for the Battle of the Wilderness that would occur the following May, and many chaplains and pastors from nearby communities led the troops in prayer and worship. In his account of the war, Gordon wrote many years later, "The religious revivals that ensued form a most remarkable and impressive chapter of war history."[3] Although Sundays remained the Lord's Day, a great many soldiers and officers—"the great body of the army" according to Gordon—met often during the rest of the week as well, sometimes for many hours.[4] It has been estimated that about 10 percent of Lee's army came to Christ during that period, roughly 7,000 men.[5]

A devout Christian himself, General Robert E. Lee encouraged the interdenominational revivals because he felt they promoted the men's welfare in this life while preparing them for the one to come. According to an account, he once saw a group of soldiers in prayer during a battle as he rode along the lines, so he dismounted, removed his hat, and went to join them. When he learned that General Stonewall Jackson had been wounded in May 1863 at the Battle of Chancellorsville, Lee sent word to his counterpart that he was praying for healing. He wrote, "When a suitable occasion offers, give him my love, and tell him that I wrestled in Prayer for him last night, as I never prayed, I believe, for myself."[6]

On both sides, among the enlisted men and officers, faith in the Lord Jesus Christ sustained thousands of men and their families during the terrible ordeal that was the American Civil War.

END NOTES

1. Janney, 86.
2. Ibid., 87–88.
3. Ibid., 89.
4. Ibid., 90.
5. Rebecca Price Janney, *Who Goes There: A Cultural History of Heaven and Hell.* (Moody Publishers, 2009), 98.
6. Ibid., 95.

January 1, 1863

The Emancipation Proclamation

ON NEW YEAR'S EVE 1862–63, President Lincoln spent a sleepless night as his mind kept turning back to the men whose lives were being poured out in battle. He had hoped to avoid war in the first place, and when it came, Lincoln desired that the South would rejoin the Union quickly, yet the conflict had resulted in a drawn-out affair with terrible loss of life and property. He told one Senator that it was a great irony that he should be cast in the role of war leader when the sight of blood made him sick, and he hated violence.[1] There was, however, something that he was determined to do, something else for which he would be remembered, and it was going to take place that very New Year's Day.

In the afternoon with officials gathered about a table, Abraham Lincoln signed the Emancipation Proclamation with a hand that trembled from standing for hours at a public reception, receiving guests. He wanted his enemies to know that he was not shaking out of indecision or fear, but that he was certain this was the right thing to do—to free the slaves who had suffered during so much of America's history. He said, "If my name ever goes into history, it will be for this act."[2]

Learning of the Proclamation, Henry Turner, a black minister, ran along Pennsylvania Avenue with a copy to read to a group gathered there, but he was so winded when he reached them that another man took the document from his hands and read it. Afterward a spontaneous celebration broke out, and they cheered Lincoln when he came to the window to watch. Turner remarked, "(N)othing like it will ever be seen again in this life."[3]

Two years later as the war reached an end, Abraham Lincoln toured the demolished Confederate capital of Richmond, Virginia with a small group of associates. They witnessed the terrible destruction, relieved beyond words that the struggle was finally ending. As they walked along the riverbank, the only people they saw were a small group of blacks digging in the ground near a house. One of them, an older man, dropped his spade and ran over to the President when he spotted their liberator. "Bless the Lord," he cried. Then he fell before Lincoln on his knees shouting, "Here is the great Messiah!" His companions gathered around the President saying similar things, much to Lincoln's distress. He begged them to get up from the ground. "Don't kneel to me," he said. "That is not right. You must kneel to God only, and thank Him for the liberty you will hereafter enjoy. I am but God's humble instrument." As they got up, Lincoln continued. "You may rest assured, that as long as I live no one shall put a shackle to your limbs, and you shall have all the rights which God has given to every other free citizen of this Republic."[4]

Before the President and his entourage left, the former slaves showed their gratitude by singing from their hearts:

Oh, all ye people clap your hands,
And with triumphant voices sing;
No force the mighty power withstands
Of God, the universal King.[5]

Realizing that Lincoln was in their midst, many more of Richmond's Negro population streamed to the site, joining in the singing. Expecting the President to say something, they looked at him with awe and thankfulness. Then he spoke once again:

My poor friends, you are free—free as air. You can cast off the name of slave and trample upon it; it will come to you no more. Liberty is your birthright. God gave it to you as He gave it to others, and it is a sin that you have been deprived of it for so many years. But you must try to deserve this priceless boon. Let the world see that you merit it, and are able to maintain it by your good works. Don't let your joy carry you into excesses. Learn the laws and obey them; obey

God's commandments and thank Him for giving you liberty; for to Him you owe all things.[6]

END NOTES

1. Stephen B. Oates, *With Malice Toward None: The Life of Abraham Lincoln.* (New York: Mentor, 1977), 360.

2. Ibid., 361.

3. Ibid., 362.

4. Janney, 90–91.

5. Ibid., 91.

6. Ibid., 92.

April 9, 1865

Surrender at Appomattox

ON SUNDAY, April 9, 1865, the war that had rent America in two drew to a close. The victorious Union General Ulysses S. Grant rode into Appomattox Courthouse, Virginia to accept the surrender of Robert E. Lee, his Confederate equal and fellow West Point graduate. Lloyd Lewis, who was present at the laying down of arms, recalled that Grant felt sad in spite of being on the winning side because, he commented, "compassion for the brave old foe drowned all the elation of his own triumph. . . ."[1]

When the men converged at a brick house at the edge of town, Grant looked more like the loser than Lee, covered with dust, wearing the disheveled coat of a private, appearing, said Lewis, "like a Missouri farmer who had by mistake crawled into a blouse that carried, unnoticed, three little silver stars on its shoulders."[2] Lee, on the other hand, carried himself as the aristocratic gentleman that he was, schooled in the old manners and customs of his native South, a region that lay in ruins. While both sides had suffered catastrophic losses, it would take the South until well into the twentieth century to recover fully from its injuries.

Lee guardedly met Grant and his staff, unsure of what further hurts would be inflicted upon his people according to the terms of surrender. In silence the Union's general wrote them down; the enlisted men were to give up their weapons while the officers could retain their own, as well as keep their property. They had permission to return to their homes without fear of being harmed by any Union soldier or government authority, in exchange for their pledge never to rebel against the United States of America again. Lee was taken aback by the generous spirit of the conditions, and Lewis recalled that his face "lit up" as he said, "This will have a very happy effect upon my army."[3] He went on to ask Grant if the Confederate soldiers could keep their horses, and Grant said that would be alright since most of them were farmers and needed the animals for their livelihoods. "At this," Lewis recorded, "Lee melted entirely. 'This will have the best possible effect upon the men. It will be very gratifying and will do much toward conciliating our people.'"[4]

There was something else on Lee's mind, however. At this point, feeling that he could speak in confidence to Grant, the older general leaned closer and quietly disclosed that his men were starving—that they had been subsisting on parched corn for several days. "It was," said Lewis, "like one brother confiding in another." Indeed it was. Although they had been mortal enemies during the war, the two men had a bond closer than national allegiance, faith in the Lord Jesus.

Grant sprang into action, directing his staff to travel throughout the Union regiments to drum up provisions for the Southerners. He told them to "ask every man who has three rations to turn over two of them. Go to the commissaries, go to the quartermasters. General Lee's army is on the point of starvation."[5]

Many Union soldiers, upon receiving word of Lee's capitulation, began to celebrate with the firing of their guns into the spring air, and Grant immediately ordered them to stop. "The rebels are our countrymen again," he said. "The best sign of rejoicing after the victory will be to abstain from all demonstrations on the field."[6]

Grant had lived out President Lincoln's assuaging message from his second inauguration weeks earlier, one based on the Chief Executive's own deep-seated faith in the Almighty:

With malice toward none; with charity for all; with firmness in the right, as God gives us to see the right, let us strive on to finish the work we are in; to bind up the nation's wounds; to care for him who shall have borne the battle, and for his widow, and his orphan— to do all which may achieve and cherish a just, and a lasting peace, among ourselves, and with all nations.[7]

END NOTES

1. Janney, 97.
2. Ibid.
3. Ibid., 98.
4. Ibid., 99.
5. Ibid.
6. Ibid.
7. Oates, 447.

April 14, 1865

The Assassination of Abraham Lincoln

The nation was just beginning to adjust to the reality that its long and devastating civil war had ended when another terrible blow struck. On the evening of April 14, Good Friday, President Lincoln went to Ford's Theater for a chance to unwind. The comic production was "Our American Cousin," but the night turned tragic when actor John Wilkes Boothe shot Lincoln as the Chief Executive sat in the Presidential Box, then fled yelling, *"Sic semper tyrannis!"* (Thus always to tyrants.) He had hoped to engage in a conspiracy to kill several other officials, including General Grant and the secretaries of state and war so that the government would be thrown into chaos, allowing the Confederacy to rise again. No such thing, happened, although Secretary of State William Seward did survive an attempt against his life that same night. Lincoln died the following morning at the age of fifty-six.

Americans wondered how this terrible thing could have happened when they had already endured four years of carnage and anguish. As was customary, they draped homes and businesses in black as a sign of public mourning, and they turned out to pay their respects by the thousands as the funeral train made its way through many towns and cities on its way to Lincoln's burial in Illinois. They also turned to God to soothe their pain. At the funeral held in the White House, Dr. Phineas D. Gurley of the New York Avenue Presbyterian Church, where Lincoln had worshiped, assured the nation that God was still sovereign and could be trusted in spite of the latest catastrophe:

> He is dead; but the God in whom he trusted lives, and He can guide and strengthen his successor, as He guided and strengthened him. He is dead; but the memory of his virtues, of his wise and patriotic counsels and labors, of his calm and steady faith in God lives, is precious, and will be a power for good in the country quite down to the end of time. He is dead; but the cause he so ardently loved, so ably, patiently, faithfully represented and defended—not for himself only, not for us only, but for all people in all their coming generations, till time shall be no more—that cause survives his fall, and will survive it.1

On Easter Sunday throughout the newly restored nation other pastors spoke of Lincoln from their pulpits. In New York the Rev. Dr. N. L. Rice reassured his congregation that in spite of the tragedy, the country could, according to Psalm 46, be still and know that God was still God. In a Lincoln funeral sermon in Philadelphia, the Rev. Phillips Brooks said, "May God make us worthy of the memory of Abraham Lincoln!" H. H. Cody captured the national mood in his song, *The Death Knell is Tolling*. It carried with it a sense that as citizens of a Christian nation, Americans were grieving hard, but not as those without hope:

> The death knell is tolling, the flag at half-mast,
> The land drap'd in mourning, we all stand aghast,
> As the tidings so fearful are borne to our ears;
> And today we are bending in sorrow and tears
> O'er a President's grave, 'round a newly wrought
>   tomb,
> Made by deeds of such darkness that horror and
>   gloom,
> Spread a pall o'er the land while a great nation
>   weeps,
> O'er the form of the dead who so peacefully sleeps.
> Yes, peacefully sleeps, heeding not the foul hand
> That is stain'd with the choicest life-blood of the
>   land,
> Heeding not the wild waves of anguish that roll

O'er the hearts of all true men, chilling the soul,
His mission accomplish'd, his life work is o'er,
The tumults of earth shall disturb him no more;
Great Martyr of Freedom! He has gone to his God,
And we're left to weep, and "Pass under the rod."

O God of our Fathers! We look up to thee;
In this hour of sadness, here bending the knee;
We crave thy protection in the midst of the gloom,
As we stand the third time, by a President's tomb;
Our way lies in darkness, and the old ship of State
Droops colors in mourning, o'er her Captain's sad fate;
But with Thee at the helm, our flag shall still wave
"O'er the land of the free, and the home of the brave."
Sleep, sleep, sleep, Lincoln sleep, sleep.

END NOTES

1. This section is adapted from Rebecca Price Janney, *Who Goes There: A Cultural History of Heaven and Hell.* (Chicago: Moody Publishers, 2009), 104–106.

1898

The Spanish-American War

BY THE 1890s Spain had been in control of the island of Cuba since the time of Christopher Columbus, but a movement towards independence was underway. Many Cubans were tired of being under that European power, and as the situation became unstable in the beginning of 1898, President McKinley ordered the battleship *Maine* to Havana. The idea was to protect U.S. interests in Cuba, particularly the multi-millions of dollars of investments that American businesses had made in sugar plantations. Then, on the night of February 15, the *Maine* suddenly and mysteriously exploded, killing over 260 men on board. Although it has never been determined exactly who might have caused the devastation, popular opinion held that Spain engineered the attack. "Remember the *Maine*" became a rallying cry in the U.S., which recognized Cuban independence and declared war on Spain in April.

President McKinley was a deeply devout Methodist who believed that America was a "city on a hill" meant to extend its democratic ideals, as well as its Christian way of life to other parts of the world. Although he initially opposed going to war against Spain, he came to view the conflict as a time in which "our aspirations as a Christian, peace-loving people will be realized."[1] Most Americans agreed with their President that Spanish rule over Cuba, as well as Puerto Rico, Guam, and the Philippines needed to end so their people could emerge from old-style Spanish rule and live instead under fresh and new Christian-based democracies.

According to *The California Christian Advocate*, "This war is the Kingdom of God coming!" *The Nation* proclaimed, "Coming to poor Cuba—the sunrise of a better day for the Philippines! . . . Oppression, cruelty, bigotry, superstition, and ignorance must down, and give a Christian civilization the right of way." The *Pacific Advocate* stated, "The cross will follow the flag. The clock of the ages is striking."[2]

Although Spain had once been a major world power, its sun was rapidly setting at the end of the nineteenth century, and the United States came out victorious by the end of that summer. When McKinley spoke to an audience of Methodists shortly afterwards, he shared his thoughts about the Spanish-American War, especially as it related to the American acquisition of the Philippines:

I am not ashamed to tell you, gentlemen, that I went down on my knees and prayed Almighty God for light and guidance more than one night. And one night late it came to me this way. . . . There was nothing left for us to do but to take them all and to educate the Filipinos and uplift and civilize and Christianize them and by God's grace do the very best we could by them, as our fellow men for whom Christ also died.[3]

END NOTES

1. Charles S. Olcott, *The Life of William McKinley*, vol. 1 (Boston: Houghton Mifflin, 1916), 19.

2. Sydney E. Ahlstrom, *A Religious History of the American People*, vol. 1 (Garden City, NY: Image Books, 1975), 879.

3. Ibid.

September 5, 1901

President McKinley's Assassination

D URING THE first year of his second term in office President McKinley traveled to Buffalo, New York for a Pan American Exposition. Late in the afternoon of September 5, he stood in a line receiving admirers when a young man approached him with a gun he had hidden under a handkerchief. He fired two shots at McKinley, grazing his shoulder with the first, and critically wounding the President with the second that entered his stomach, colon, and kidneys. As guards wrestled Leon Czolgosz, President McKinley managed to conduct himself in a manner worthy of the gospel that he had followed since boyhood. He implored those detaining Czolgosz not to be cruel to him, and while preparing to go under anesthesia for emergency surgery a short time later, the President calmly recited the Lord's Prayer.

Initially, McKinley's prospects for a full recovery looked good, but a few days later, his health began to deteriorate when gangrene set in. When he realized that he was going to die, the President reassured his stricken wife that God would take care of them both. He whispered to her, "God's will, not ours, be done," and she quietly murmured, "For his sake. For his sake," as she took his hands and tried to smile through her tears. McKinley's final words were, "Goodbye, all; good-bye. It is God's way. His will be done." Then he recited words from a favorite hymn, "Nearer my God to Thee, nearer to Thee."[1]

The Rev. W. H. Chapman presided over a service for the President at the Metropolitan Methodist Church in Washington, D.C. in which he spoke of McKinley's strongly held Christian beliefs:

> How peaceful and resigned he went into the valley, covered with splendid sunshine, and found rest from his labors! He has left behind him, to his kindred and to us the rich legacy of a splendid character and an unsullied record. A life that says to others: "This is the way. Walk in it, the way that leads to moral wealth, far above all material wealth, and which leads at last to heaven and to God."

> We shall miss him in this sanctuary and look no more upon him in yonder pew devotional in worship and listening attentively to the precious word as if indeed

it were manna to his soul and a refreshing stream from the fountain of life. But he worshiped today in the temple not made with hands, with many of those with whom he was wont to worship in the church below. May we all imitate his example, emulate his virtues and at the last be counted worthy of a place with him in the kingdom of heaven.[2]

In a eulogy on September 19, the Honorable John W. Griggs, who had served as United States Attorney General under McKinley, also spoke about his deep spiritual character:

But if President McKinley was noble in his life, in his death he was sublime.

"He taught us how to live, (and O, too high the price of knowledge), taught us how to die." Shall we not rather see in him a manifestation of the greatness and the purity to which the Divine spirit that is in man may attain when restrained and guided by the Divine standards? Shall we not hope, nay, believe! That, in a wider sphere, in a fairer land, his spirit still lives and labors and loves?

When darkness of death was settling over him he murmured words of rest and home. I think that when the light of the eternal morning greeted his soul's eyes, he knew that he had found them—rest and home.[3]

END NOTES

1. This section is adapted from Rebecca Price Janney, *Who Goes There? A Cultural History of Heaven and Hell.* (Chicago: Moody Publishers, 2009), 136–38.

2. Ibid.

3. Ibid.

December 17, 1903

The Wright Brothers' First Successful Flight

THE WRIGHT brothers, Wilbur and Orville, spent most of their early lives in Dayton, Ohio where their father, Milton, was a Bishop in the Church of the Brethren in Christ. Bishop Wright believed in engaging the mind as well as the spirit and as a result, his boys got involved in all sorts of experiments from creating a machine that folded newspapers to making higher flying kites and sleds that ran faster than the norm. An important leader in his denomination, Wright often traveled, and in 1878 after one trip, he returned home with a toy helicopter for his boys. Eleven year-old Wilbur and his seven year-old brother were fascinated with the device, spending long hours with it, but when it finally broke, they decided to make one of their own design. In their later years, both men agreed that it was the one toy that most influenced their path in life. From then on, they dreamed of creating a machine that would one day enable people to fly.

As a young man, Wilbur had planned to attend Harvard, but he became withdrawn after an ice hockey accident knocked out several teeth. Instead, he assisted his father in his church work while nursing his mother, who had tuberculosis, and when his little brother Orville opened a print shop, Wilbur joined him. In the 1890s bicycles came to national attention, and the brothers started a sales and repair shop instead, using money from this business to fund their passion for aeronautics. Wilbur was at the forefront of the venture. They read about others who were trying to fly and researched various designs and methods related to flight so that by 1900 they were experimenting with gliders on the North Carolina coast, in Kitty Hawk, where there were regular wind patterns and dunes that would make crash landings less traumatic. Needing a glider that could lift as well as be controlled, the Wright brothers worked for three years on their aircraft and its components, even to the point of building a wind tunnel to conduct further experiments after their first season in North Carolina didn't work out. By December 1903, they were ready to fly, but difficulties related to propeller shafts and weather dogged them.

At 10:30 on the morning of December 17, 1903, Wilbur and Orville Wright decided it was time to try, although it was a risky proposition. With the bitter wind blowing steadily at thirty miles per hour, it felt like four degrees in the coastal town. The weather had been more favorable at the beginning of that week, but the bachelors observed the Sabbath and wouldn't fly on a Sunday. With each day conditions worsened, and they realized that if they didn't try at that time, they wouldn't make it back home for Christmas. At 10:35 with winds at twenty-seven miles per hour, Orville took the flyer up in the air for twelve seconds, traveling 120 feet. By noon, the brothers were taking the aircraft on its fourth flight, this time going 852 feet in just under one minute. "Those first few flights were where physics and faith, engineering and poetry all came together. It was the Wright brothers' time and they rose to the occasion."[1]

END NOTES

1. Wright Brothers Areoplane Co. of Dayton, Ohio, http:// www.first-to-fly.com/.

April 18, 1906

The San Francisco Earthquake

IN 1906 the modern Pentecostal movement began on Azusa Street in Los Angeles, with 300 to 1500 people gathering at one time to worship. Distinguished by speaking in tongues, miraculous healings, and prophetic utterances that ushered in a new epoch of Christian history, one that had actually begun with the very first Christians when the Holy Spirit came upon them. According to some accounts, during the Los Angeles revival, a young participant prophesied that a tremendous earthquake was going to happen in the coming days.

Before dawn on Wednesday, April 18, 1906, a horrific 7.7 magnitude earthquake shook the city of San Francisco— some scientists believe it may have actually hit 8.3. Not only did it bring down buildings, it also set off a chain of fires that ended in the worst urban conflagration in the nation's history, including the disastrous 1871 Chicago Fire. The blaze raged for three days, consuming nearly five hundred city blocks and killing upwards of seven hundred people. Out of a population of 400,000, 250,000 of them lost their homes.

Pietro Toresani, an Italian immigrant living in San Francisco, woke up abruptly at 5:12 a.m. on that ill-fated morning in 1906. "There was a big noise as if it was made by the devil," he wrote in a journal. "There was a concert of bottles, 40 glasses, a mandolin and a guitar." He staggered out of his bed and wandered outside where he said, "I lost courage and patience and evoking 'mommy' and 'daddy' repeatedly . . . I threw myself again to the ground as if I had a disease, as if I was drunk. . . . Like a crazy man I was looking here and there at an infinity of dead bodies horribly squashed."

W. E. Alexander recalled how he was literally shaken by the quake, "until I thought my teeth would come out," while his bed jumped about.

I never felt so small and helpless in my life as I did that morning when I gazed upon the stricken city. . . . When I looked out, the pale moon was shining through the smoke from the fires just starting and I halted in surprise, thinking, I suppose, that she should not be there; that by all tokens, she should have been shaken from her position and lain shattered and broken at our feet. We then went up on our roof and found that the fires were making great headway and my wife's first remark was, "The city is doomed—no power on Earth can save it."

Many people organized their bewildered thoughts along religious lines; it was, after all, an event of "biblical proportions." A man named G. A. Raymond wandered around, trying to make sense of the terror as morning broke:

> Outside I witnessed a sight I never want to see again. It was dawn and light. I looked up. The air was filled with falling stones. People around me were crushed to death on all sides. All around the huge buildings were shaking and waving. Every moment there were reports like 100 cannons going off at one time. Then streams of fire would shoot out, and other reports followed.
>
> I asked a man standing next to me what happened. Before he could answer a thousand bricks fell on him and he was killed. A woman threw her arms around my neck. I pushed her away and fled. All around me buildings were rocking and flames shooting. As I ran people on all sides were crying, praying and calling for help. I thought the end of the world had come.[1]

END NOTES

1. This section was adapted from Rebecca Price Janney, *Who Goes There: A Cultural History of Heaven and Hell*, (Chicago: Moody Publishers, 2009), 127–29.

April 1912

The Sinking of the Titanic

MANY PEOPLE at the beginning of the twentieth century believed that the new era would be
the start of unprecedented peace and human
progress. Particularly in the West, so many advances were
being made in education, morals, technology, and science that
it seemed that before too long, poverty, ignorance, sickness,
and war would be eliminated. A major symbol of human
development was a colossal ship called *RMS Titanic*, a lux-
ury liner whose route would be Southampton, England to
New York. The craft boasted unparalleled opulence for its
first class passengers, including a swimming pool, a Turkish
bath, and the finest food and décor. It didn't, however, have
many lifeboats, just enough for one-third of its passengers.
Perhaps one reason for this was the absolute confidence that

its builders had in the *Titanic*. According to *Shipbuilder* magazine, the vessel was "practically unsinkable." A deckhand who was trying to convince an anxious passenger not to worry said, "Not even God could sink her."[1]

On April 10, 2,240 people embarked on the *Titanic* where a party atmosphere held sway in the excitement of this grand liner's maiden journey across the sea. Just before midnight on the night of the fifteenth, passengers who were still awake felt a small bump, but they didn't become concerned until they could no longer hear the constant sound of the engines. The ship had struck an iceberg in the North Atlantic, and it didn't take long for the captain to realize how grave the situation was. He ordered the ship's band to play lively tunes to keep up the spirits of the passengers, but when everyone understood that the ship was going to sink, the music turned to hymns of the Christian faith. Two hours and forty minutes after the ship struck the iceberg, the *Titanic* slipped under the water, taking over 1,500 people with it. There were 705 survivors.

Evangelist John Harper was on board that night, and he hurried to put his six-year-old daughter in one of the lifeboats. That accomplished, he went throughout the vessel warning people of its demise and telling them that in order to avoid spiritual death, they needed to put their faith in Jesus Christ for the forgiveness of their sins. When he could no longer stay on board the sinking ship, Harper jumped into the frigid water and took hold of a piece of debris. Spotting another passenger, he asked the man if he knew Christ.

When the man said he did not, Harper told him how he could. The man of God met his Maker that night and likely took several people to heaven along with him.[2]

END NOTES

1. Rev. Dr. James Galyon, comment on "Not even God could sink her!" 2 Worlds Collide Blog, comment posted on April 14, 2007, http://www.drjamesgalyon.wordpress.com/2007/04/14/" not-even-god-could-sink-her"/.

2. Glimpses of Christian History, April 15, 1912, "While Unsinkable' *Titanic* Sank, John Harper Preached," http:// chi.gospelcom.net/DAILYF/2003/04/daily-04-15-2003.shtml.

1914–1918

World War One: "The War to End All Wars"

IN SARAJEVO on a June morning in 1914, a young Bosnian Serb named Gavrilo Princep fired at the visting Archduke Franz Ferdinand and his wife, the Duchess Sophie Chotek, as they rode by in an official motorcade. Both the heir apparent to the throne of the Hapsburg Empire and his wife died in the attack, an event that touched off a series of European political and military alliances so that by summer's end, the continent was immersed in war. Most observers were cavalier about the conflict, maintaining that by Christmas their opponents would have been soundly thrashed. Instead, the European nations brought themselves to the brink of utter chaos and desolation, and by the spring of 1917, the United States entered the war in order to put those nations out of their intense misery and give them a sound footing for the future.

During the four-year war, people around the world were shocked at the horrors wrought by the hostilities, particularly at the way in which innovative technologies enabled nations to ravage their opponents. New to warfare were submarines, airplanes, mechanized tanks, machine guns, and poison gas. People became slaves to rather than masters of the weapons they had created.[1] By the end of the conflict, much of Europe lay in ruins. Russia had undergone a bloody internal revolution that brought about the fall of the Czar and the beginning of the communist Soviet Union. It also buried two-and-a-half million soldiers and some 20 percent of its civilians. Statistically, for each day of World War I, 6,000 Europeans died. Of the nearly three million Americans who served in Europe, 115,000 did not return.[2]

Each American soldier who stepped on a troop ship as he prepared for war was given a New Testament provided by the New York Bible Society. In it a message from former President Theodore Roosevelt was inscribed, encouraging the men, "*Love mercy*; treat your enemies well; succor the afflicted; treat every woman as if she were your sister; care for the little children; and be tender with the old and helpless. *Walk humbly*; you will do so if you study the life and teachings of the Savior, walking in His steps."[3] He reflected the belief that stretched all the way back to the Pilgrims and Puritans that America needed to set an example for other nations and peoples who had lost their way in a darkened world.

Of the millions of soldiers who read that message, Floyd Horton was a young man from Illinois who experienced firsthand the travails of the war "over there" in Europe. He recalled years later that when he reached France, he couldn't believe how stark the country was, that he had never seen the likes of it. When he reached Verdun, Horton became engaged in some of the most intense fighting of the war, and in the battle, he was shot in the arm. Although he was losing blood and traumatized, the Midwesterner had no choice but to walk an uncomfortable distance to an ambulance, then it took awhile before the emergency vehicle could safely leave the area. Following a difficult ride, they actually made it to a field hospital. Horton was ready for some loving care and that is what awaited him. He never forgot how members of a different kind of Army awaited him; The Salvation Army was at the hospital, its officers dispensing doughnuts, coffee, and tenderness to the wounded, living out former President Roosevelt's exhortation to love mercy and walk humbly with their God.

END NOTES

1. Rebecca Price Janney, *Great Stories in American History.* (Camp Hill, PA: Horizon Books, 1998), 111–12.
2. Ibid., 112.
3. Ibid., 114–15.

October 29, 1929

The Stock Market Crash

IN AMERICA the decade after World War I is remembered as "the roaring twenties," a time of burgeoning world influence and wealth. The population stretched to well over one hundred million, unemployment hovered around 5 percent, illiteracy was on the decline, the standard of living was improving, and the nation was on the move, enjoying the benefits of mass produced automobiles. Herbert Hoover's 1928 Presidential slogan promised "a chicken in every pot and a car in every garage." He told the country, "We in America are nearer to the final triumph over poverty than ever before in the history of any land. . . . We have not reached the goal, but, given a chance to go forward with the policies of the last eight years, we shall soon with the help of God be in sight of the day when poverty will be banished from this nation."[1]

It seemed there wasn't anything that good old Yankee inge-
nuity couldn't solve, and the stock market reached euphorically
high levels. Then came weeks of instability on Wall Street in
the fall of 1929, ending on Black Tuesday, October 29 when
the market went into a slide that lasted for a month, then crash-
landed into the start of the Great Depression of the 1930s. The
Dow Jones Industrial Average did not reach pre-October 29th
levels again until the 1950s. By 1933, one-fourth of the
American workforce was unemployed.

The economic upheaval was ruinous for many people,
including James Cash Penney, who had built a successful business called the Golden Rule Stores that he based on Jesus'
teaching to treat others the way you would want others to
treat you. During the Depression, Penney's investments
soured. He lost his worldly goods, his health, and his family.
He considered suicide. Coming alongside him, a friend
encouraged Penney to enter a sanitarium for rest, and while
he was there his health began to improve. What provided the
greatest healing, however, occurred early one morning while
he was taking a walk before breakfast. He heard people down
the hall singing a hymn that he remembered from childhood
and drawing closer, he found a group of doctors and nurses
worshiping in the chapel. They sang:

Be not dismayed whate'er betide,
God will take care of you
All you need he will provide
God will take care of you. [2]

He decided to join them, and when someone read from the book of Matthew, "Come unto me all ye that labour and are heavy laden, and I will give you rest" (Matthew 11:28 KJV), Penney had a personal revelation. He realized that while he'd been motivated all his life to honor God with his hard work, it was time to rest in his grace instead.

"At that time something happened to me which I cannot explain," he recalled when looking back on the experience. He cried out to God, asking if he would take care of him, knowing that he could no longer live in his own strength.

"I felt I was passing out of darkness into light," he said as he sensed the Lord telling him, "only believe." It was no longer about his own efforts, but God's. "In the midst of failure to believe, I was being helped back to believing," he said. "It was a life-changing miracle, and I've been a different person ever since. I saw God in his glory and planned to be baptized and to join a church."[3]

By the mid-1930s, Penney's finances began to turn around, even as his personal life did, and his J.C. Penney Department Stores became a fixture in American life. Penny donated large sums of money to various charities and missions before his death at the age of ninety-five.

END NOTES

1. Samuel Eliot Morison and Henry Steele Commager, *The Growth of the American Republic, Volume Two.* (New York: Oxford University Press, 1962), 644.

2. Glimpses of Christian History, Glimpses #178: "J. C. Pen-

ney and the Business of Being Christian," http://chi.gospelcom. net/GLIMPSEF/Glimpses/glmps178.shtml..

3. Ibid.

4. Ibid.

December 7, 1941

Pearl Harbor: "A Date Which Will Live in Infamy"

AT SUNRISE on December 7, 1941, Mitsuo Fuchida led a squadron of Japanese planes toward Hawaii's Hickam Field. There at Pearl Harbor the entire Pacific Fleet slumbered under the promise of a brilliant sky, a treat for sailors who had come from the wintry U.S. mainland. At 7:49 a.m., Fuchida's cry, "Tora, Tora, Tora!" reverberated from his microphone into the planes of 360 other Japanese air warriors, and like mechanical wasps, they dive-bombed eight battleships, obliterating two and inflicting major damage upon six others. Nearly a dozen other ships, cruisers, minelayers, and destroyers bobbed about powerlessly in water slick with burning oil. The enemy shattered one hundred and fifty planes as well. More than two thousand servicemen died that morning, and over a thousand were wounded.

After World War II had broken out in Europe in September, 1939, Japan announced its support for Germany and Italy, plunging its relationship with America into a deep well of suspicion and resentment. Many American leaders worried that the Japanese wanted to attack both U.S. Pacific territories and friendly nations, but they never imagined the scale of destruction that rained upon Pearl Harbor or the brashness of the plot itself. On that December morning, Japanese forces took less than two hours to crush the U.S. Pacific Fleet.

The following day, President Franklin D. Roosevelt appeared before Congress seeking a formal declaration of war as millions of Americans listened on the radio. In one of his most famous speeches, the President assured lawmakers and the American public that God would help the country:

> Yesterday, December 7, 1941— a date which will live in infamy— the United States of America was suddenly and deliberately attacked by naval and air forces of the Empire of Japan. . .
>
> Yesterday the Japanese Government also launched an attack against Malaya.
>
> Last night Japanese forces attacked Hong Kong.
>
> Last night Japanese forces attacked Guam.
>
> Last night Japanese forces attacked the Philippine Islands.

Last night the Japanese attacked Wake Island. And this morning the Japanese attacked Midway Island ...

Japan has, therefore, undertaken a surprise offensive extending throughout the Pacific area. The facts of yesterday and today speak for themselves. The people of the United States have already formed their opinions and well understand the implications to the very life and safety of our Nation ...

With confidence in our armed forces—with the unbounding determination of our people—we will gain the inevitable triumph—so help us God.

I ask that the Congress declare that since the unprovoked and dastardly attack by Japan on Sunday, December 7, 1941, a state of war has existed between the United States and the Japanese Empire.[1]

Three days later, Japan's friends—Germany and Italy—declared war on America, which was now fully immersed in the tides of World War II.

END NOTES

1. Franklin Delano Roosevelt Presidential Library and Museum, December 8, 1941—"Franklin Roosevelt Asks Congress for a Declaration of War with Japan," http://www.fdrlibrary. marist.edu/tmirhdee.html

June 6, 1944

D-Day

IN 1943 in London, General Sir Frederick Morgan began planning an Allied invasion of the European continent to free its oppressed and suffering people from Adolf Hitler, whose Nazi forces were stretched thinly over three fronts. In addition, discord among Hitler's senior officers was taking its toll.

The German dictator prepared for an Allied landing by laying mines and other underwater obstacles in the English Channel, along with barbed wire and artillery emplacements along the beaches. He sent most of his divisions to the Pas de Calais where he believed the assault would take place, but the Allies, under General Dwight D. Eisenhower, actually were bound for Normandy to the south.

The night before, General Eisenhower visited some of the soldiers who were scheduled to invade Normandy, asking

about their personal lives, where they were from, what kind
of jobs they did. He was obviously bowed down with the
weight of knowing that many of the young men would never
see their families again after Operation Overlord, as it was
called. One paratrooper sought to ease Eisenhower's concern.
"Now quit worrying, General," he said. "We'll take care of this
thing for you."[1]

In his invasion field order, the General outlined how difficult their mission was going to be. He also encouraged the
soldiers to rely upon God for strength to go through with it
saying, "Your enemy is well trained, well equipped and battle-
hardened. He will fight savagely. . . . (Therefore) beseech the
blessings of Almighty God on this great and noble undertaking."[2] Back home on that day, people went to their churches
to pray for the brave men facing Hitler's troops, and President Roosevelt also led them in a time of intercession:

> Almighty God: Our sons, pride of our nation, this
> day have set upon a mighty endeavor, a struggle to
> preserve our Republic, our religion and our civiliza-
> tion, and to set free a suffering humanity. Lead them
> straight and true; give strength to their arms, stout-
> ness to their hearts, steadfastness in their faith. They
> will need Thy blessings.
>
> Their road will be long and hard. For the enemy
> is strong. He may hurl back our forces. They will be
> sore tried, by night and by day . . . The darkness will
> be rent by noise and flame. Men's souls will be shaken

with the violence of war ... Success may not come with rushing speed, but we shall return again and again; and we know by Thy grace, and by the righteousness of our cause, our sons will triumph.

Some will never return. Embrace these, Father, and receive them, Thy heroic servants, into Thy kingdom.

And for us at home—fathers, mothers, children, wives, sisters and brothers of brave men overseas, whose thoughts and prayers are ever with them—help us, Almighty God, to rededicate ourselves in renewed faith in Thee in this hour of great sacrifice ...[3]

Around midnight of June 6, 1944, the Allied air attack began, followed by an amphibious landing in waters so rough that the Germans didn't think the assault would happen on that day. Over 130,000 men landed—the biggest single day invasion ever— and nearly 5,000 Americans died.

END NOTES

1. Rebecca Price Janney, *Great Stores in American History*. (Camp Hill, PA: Horizon Books, 1998), 137.
2. Ibid.
3. Ibid., 137–38.

August 6, 1945

The First Atomic Bomb is Dropped

GERMANY FOUGHT intensely to retain command of Europe, but D-Day and the ensuing battles destroyed the Third Reich, a power that Hitler had once predicted would rule for a thousand years. Germany admitted defeat in May of 1945.

At the Potsdam conference near Berlin in July, President Harry Truman and British Prime Minister Winston Churchill issued an ultimatum to the Japanese—surrender unconditionally at once, and return all of its conquests made since the end of the nineteenth century. If they did so, the Allies would occupy Japan without making them subservient, for as long as it took them to form a peaceful, non-aggressive government. If the answer was "no," the United States and its Allies would bring about "prompt and utter destruction."[1] Japan chose the latter.

On August 6 the B-29 *Enola Gay* dropped a new and terrible bomb on Hiroshima, a major Japanese industrial hub. The entire Second Japanese Army perished in the blast, four square miles of the city were decimated, and over 60,000 people were killed. When Japan still refused to capitulate, a second atom bomb was employed, against Nagasaki, on August 9. In that explosion, 36,000 more people perished. On August 14, Japan at last surrendered.

Mitsuo Fuchida, who had commanded the Japanese attack on Pearl Harbor, was stationed in Hiroshima that fateful August, and just hours before the *Enola Gay* unleashed its horror, the pilot left for another military base, the second time during the war that he had narrowly escaped with his life. The first had been at the Battle of Midway.

When the end of the war came, Fuchida's illustrious career as a pilot ended with the dismantling of his country's armed forces. Although he tried to make his way as a farmer, he was unable to put the war behind him, nor could he figure out why his life had been spared twice. General Douglas MacArthur called him before the Tokyo war crimes trials several times. On one of those occasions, Fuchida saw an American handing out pamphlets at a train station. He took one and immediately became interested in the title, "I Was a Prisoner of Japan." In it was the story of Jake DeShazer, who had been part of a surprise raid on Tokyo in April 1942. Full of revenge for what had happened at Pearl Harbor, DeShazer enjoyed bombing the Japanese city, but he didn't count on being captured. He spent the rest of the war as a prisoner, being mistreated, nursing intense hatred for America's enemy.

After two years DeShazer was permitted to read a Bible, and he came to realize that Christ was his only hope. He trained as a missionary after the war and returned to the land and people he once had despised to tell them about the Lord Jesus. Fuchida found this story unforgettable, and he bought a Bible to see for himself if the Gospel might be true. It was then that he came to understand the meaning of Christ's death, and he asked for forgiveness for his sins, promising to become a strong Christian with a purpose in living rather than a bitter former pilot. Fuchida went on to become an evangelist.

He once said, "I would give anything to retract my actions . . . at Pearl Harbor, but it is impossible. Instead, I now work at striking the death-blow to the basic hatred which infests the human heart and causes such tragedies. And that hatred cannot be uprooted without assistance from Jesus Christ."[2] God not only brought peace to a war-weary world, but also to the souls of two mortal enemies who had fought in it.

END NOTES

1. Morison and Commager, 843. (1961 edition)
2. "Mitsuo Fuchida: The Enemy Whose Attack Provoked America," The Christian History Institute, http://chi.gospelcom .net/kids/glimpsesforkids/gfk029_2.php

1954

Supreme Court Decision: Brown v. Board of Education of Topeka, Kansas

THROUGHOUT the post-World War II South, *Jim Crow* laws that stretched back to the last half of the nineteenth century existed, regulations that segregated blacks from whites in public places. They dictated that the races were to employ "separate but equal" facilities, but whatever "nod to fairness" it may have represented in no way mirrored reality. In Topeka, Kansas in the late 1940s, there were eighteen public schools for white children but only four for blacks, hardly an equal opportunity system. Likewise, most churches were segregated, as were public washrooms, hotels, and restaurants, recreational venues, even water fountains. When President Harry Truman ordered the U.S. military to desegregate in 1948, it opened the possibility of other areas of equal access as well, including public education.

In 1951, Oliver Brown of Topeka and two hundred other plaintiffs from five different states brought a case against public school segregation that eventually made it to the Supreme Court. Led by Chief Justice Earl Warren, the Court determined in 1954 in a watershed case that racial segregation "violates the fourteenth amendment to the U.S. Constitution, which guarantees all citizens equal protection of the laws."[1]

The following year, Val J. Washington, Director of the Republican National Committee, released a report of the progress that President Dwight Eisenhower's administration had made in the sphere of civil rights. President Eisenhower answered Mr. Washington's summation with his own letter. In it he said:

> ... the Republican Party has been firm in its insistence that there can only be one class of citizenship and has been effective in its practice of this conviction; thereby it has proved itself, in our day, a vigorous and productive champion of the ideals and purposes of Lincoln.

> ... But I am sure, the major credit must go to the people of the United States. Their sense of fair play, their recognition that all our citizens are bound in a common destiny, their spiritual faith in the dignity of all men under God—these deeply rooted characteristics of the American people are the ultimate source of the achievement reported by you.[2]

On March 26, 1956, President Eisenhower wrote to the Rev. Billy Graham asking if he could use his influence among Southern clergy to drum up grassroots support for desegregation in the South. A native North Carolinian, Graham had refused to hold segregated evangelistic crusades in that region. He eagerly responded to the President:

> I feel with you that the Church must take a place of spiritual leadership in this crucial matter that confronts not only the South but the entire nation. You will be interested to know that I am taking immediate steps to call the outstanding leaders of the major Southern denominations together as soon as possible in Atlanta for a conference on this subject. I shall outline to them your suggestions for racial understanding and progress. In addition, I will do all in my power to urge Southern ministers to call upon the people for moderation, charity, compassion and progress toward compliance with the Supreme Court decision.[3]

END NOTES

1. "Brown v. Board of Education: About the Case," Brown Foundation, http://www.brownvboard.org/summary.

2. Dwight D. Eisenhower letter to Val J. Washington, August 1, 1955, The Dwight D. Eisenhower Presidential Library and Museum, http://www.eisenhower.archives.gov/dl/Civil_Rights_Eisenhower_Administration/RNCNEWsRelease9Aug5 5pg1.pdf

3. Billy Graham letter to Dwight D. Eisenhower, March 27, 1956, Ibid., http://www.eisenhower.archives.gov/dl/Civil_ Rights_Eisenhower_Administration/LtrGraham%20toDDE27M arch56pg1.pdf

December 1955

Civil Rights Movement: Rosa Parks Refuses to
Give Up Her Seat on a Public Bus

A S A RESULT of *Brown v. Board of Education,*
African-Americans throughout the South anticipated that a new day was coming, a time in which
the races would enjoy equality in every respect. Segregation
in areas other than public education began to be challenged,
and on a December afternoon in 1955, a middle-aged woman
from Montgomery, Alabama provided a further catalyst to
action. Rosa Parks worked as a seamstress at the Montgomery Fair Department Store, and following an arduous day
of operating a hefty commercial steam press, she looked forward to getting on the bus to go home. That simple act would
alter history.

The first bus that swung into view was so crowded that
Mrs. Parks decided to wait for the next one and get a little

Christmas shopping done in the meantime. Although there were plenty of seats on the second bus, she cringed when she saw that the driver was J.F. Blake, who was known for knocking her people around. A dozen years earlier, he'd kicked her off his bus when she declined to re-enter from the back. She had studiously avoided being around him since that time, but on this day she was too tired to wait for yet another bus.

The first ten rows were for white passengers, the next twenty-six for blacks, but it was understood, and accepted, that at any time and for any reason, people of color would have to give up their seats for whites if so requested. Mrs. Parks chose a spot in in her section. Several stops later, a white man boarded and, finding no seats in his section, appealed to Blake for help. The gruff bus driver ordered the blacks to move back so the white man wouldn't have to sit next to them. Blake's temper gathered steam when no one moved. "You all better make it light on yourselves and let me have those seats," he warned.[1]

Three people moved further to the back. Rosa Parks stayed put. She had been deferring to white people all her life, and something inside told her not to take it anymore. Her grandfather, a former slave, had helped raise Rosa as a little girl, and he taught her constantly over the years that blacks were as good as any white person. Now she was willing to defend that principle. When Blake pulled the bus over and stormed down the aisle to confront her, Mrs. Parks politely refused to leave her seat, persisting even after the driver threatened to call the police. When he did so, Blake pointed an accusing finger at his recalcitrant passenger.

One officer asked, "Why haven't you obeyed the law?"

"I felt I shouldn't have to," she replied. "Why do you push us around?"

The senior policeman asked if Blake wished to press charges, and when he answered in the affirmative, they escorted the woman off the bus. As a result of the incident in which Parks was fingerprinted, photographed, and fined ten dollars, the African-American clergy of Montgomery sprang into action, led by a young pastor, Martin Luther King, Jr. They declared a strike against the bus company on December 5, one that lasted for over a year. During that time King was arrested, along with other boycott leaders, and the KKK bombed the pastor's house.

Policemen routinely harassed black motorists for the most trivial and fabricated offenses.

Both Rosa Parks and her husband lost their jobs because of their involvement in the boycott. It was a hardship to the entire black community. Their churches contributed Sunday offerings to help offset the expense of providing transportation to their members. Some insisted that violence was in order, but King preached a consistent message that Christian love alone would overcome racial prejudice and hatred.

The boycott brought the Montgomery bus system to its knees, and on December 20, 1956, it desegregated after the Supreme Court ruled that to do otherwise was unconstitutional.

Of Rosa Parks, Martin Luther King, Jr. once said,

"Nobody can doubt the depth of her Christian commitment and devotion to the teachings of Jesus ..."[2]

END NOTES

1. Adapted from Rebecca Price Janney, *Great Women in American History*. (Camp Hill, PA: Horizon Books, 1996), 157–166.

2. Mary Hull, *Rosa Parks: Civil Rights Leader*. (New York: Chelsea House Publishers, 1994), 74.

October 4, 1957

Sputnik Satellite is Launched

FOR THE SAKE of defeating Adolf Hitler, the United States and the Russians became allies during World War II. Shortly after that conflict ended, however, the two nations experienced a breach in their wartime coalition when the Soviet Union blockaded the sections of Berlin that were under its control from those under Western jurisdiction. It quickly became clear that the Russians, led by Premier Joseph Stalin, wanted to dominate all of Eastern Europe, making it communist. Winston Churchill described what was happening in a 1946 speech when he said an "iron curtain" had descended across the Continent. Under his cruel leadership, Stalin oversaw the deaths of some twenty million people whom he regarded as political enemies; some scholars say the number is actually much higher.

When the Russians acquired nuclear weapons, the U.S. was understandably anxious. What if, many worried, they used this considerable military strength to impose communism on Americans? It didn't help when Stalin's successor, Nikita Khrushchev, told a group of Western diplomats in 1956, "Whether you like it or not, history is on our side. We will bury you!"[1]

Most Americans believed that they had to stay stronger than the Soviet Union economically, scientifically, and militarily so that the country never succumbed to communism. It came as a nasty jolt, therefore, when the Russians successfully launched the first artificial satellite into space on October 4, 1957. Many worried that the enemy had developed the capacity to spy on America from space, and perhaps even to someday discharge nuclear weapons from that lofty height. It was, indeed, a watershed event. An NBC news announcer introduced the beeping of *Sputnik* with, "Listen now, for the sound that forevermore separates the old from the new."[2]

Writer Tom Wolfe observed that at the time, "Nothing less than control of the heavens was at stake. (*Sputnik*) was Armageddon, the final and decisive battle between good and evil."[3]

As *Sputnik* orbited the earth, many Americans went outside at night to try and catch a glimpse of it orbiting overhead. Teenager Homer Hickam, Jr. of Coalwood, West Virginia remembered the night vividly and what it came to mean for the course of his entire life.

I saw the bright little ball, moving majestically across the narrow star field between the ridgelines. I stared at it with no less rapt attention than if it had been God Himself in a golden chariot riding overhead. It soared with what seemed to me inexorable and dangerous purpose, as if there were no power in the universe that could stop it. All my life, everything important that had ever happened had always happened somewhere else. But Sputnik was right there in front of my eyes in my backyard in Coalwood, McDowell County, West Virginia, U.S.A. I couldn't believe it.[4]

Hickam eventually wrote about that seminal experience in his memoir *Rocket Boys*. He also went on to work for NASA training astronauts for space shuttle flights.

In November, the Soviets launched a second satellite. *Sputnik I* had spent itself by the end of October, disintegrating as it plunged back to earth. The United States, in the meantime, was rushing to get its own satellite into space, a feat that occurred on December 19, one that conveyed a far different message to the world than the Soviets. For thirteen days after its launch, SCORE (Signal Communications Orbit Relay Equipment) broadcast a tape-recorded Christmas greeting from President Eisenhower that used the ancient words of Scripture to show that America's reason for being in space was a peaceful one:

This is the President of the United States speaking.
Through the marvels of scientific advance, my voice is
coming to you from a satellite circling in outer space.
My message is a simple one. Through this unique
means I will convey to you and to all mankind America's wish for peace on Earth and goodwill toward men
everywhere.[5]

END NOTES

1. "We Will Bury You!" *Time* Magazine, November 16, 1956.

2. "The Space Race Revisited," October 2, 1997, PBS, http://
www.pbs.org/newshour/bb/science/july-dec97/sputnik_10-2
.html

3. Paul Dickson, *Sputnik: The Shock of the Century.* (New York:
Walker Publishing, 2001), 134.

4. "Sputnik and the Crisis that Followed," U.S. Centennial of
Flight Commission, http://www.centennialofflight.gov/essay/
SPACEFLIGHT/Sputnik/SP16.htm

5. Dickson, 200.

October 1962

The Cuban Missile Crisis

THROUGHOUT the late 1950s and into the early 60s America "fought" the Cold War against the communist Soviet Union. In fact, the confrontation of wills would last all the way until 1991. The two nations jockeyed with each other for superiority in the race to put men in orbit and eventually, on the moon. They also built up enormous caches of conventional and nuclear weapons, just in case, and formed alliances with other nations who shared their political philosophy. The U.S. cried "foul" each time the U.S.S.R. exerted itself against other countries to extend Russia's political power and philosophy, but no case rattled American nerves as much as Soviet influence on Cuba.

In 1959, Fidel Castro had led a revolution there, overthrowing the government of Fulgencio Batista and within a short time, he ushered in Marxist rule. Castro became allies with the Russians, and Americans found it both intolerable as well as alarming that a communist government could exist just ninety miles south of Florida.

In early October, 1962, President John F. Kennedy discovered through military reconnaissance flights that the Soviets were building missile bases in Cuba, sites intended to accommodate medium and long range intercontinental ballistic missiles. When the President addressed the nation on the evening of October 22, his news about what was going on in Cuba panicked U.S. citizens. The President declared, "It shall be the policy of this nation to regard any nuclear missile launched from Cuba against any nation in the Western Hemisphere as an attack on the United States, requiring a full retaliatory response upon the Soviet Union."[1] In addition, he announced a blockade against any Soviet ships bound for Cuba containing weapons.

During the following week, Americans prepared themselves for the possibility of a nuclear war with Russia. Schools conducted air raid drills and taught children how to find their way quickly to bomb shelters or duck under their desks for protection in the event of an atomic blast. The military stood on full alert, ready to let U.S. bombs drop on the Russians if given the command by the President. Many people prayed for deliverance, although a lot of Christians around the country believed that earth's final battle, Armageddon, was at hand.

That Sunday, October 28, pastors addressed the missile crisis in their sermons, and there were abundant references to the possibility that this was the end of the world and would bring about Christ's return. Billy Graham was preaching at a crusade in Argentina at the time, and he addressed his audience on the night of the 28th, after it became known that war would be averted because the Soviets agreed to pull their missiles out of Cuba. Graham said,

> Many think this may be the prelude to the greatest crisis in the history of mankind. Never before have weapons of such magnitude been poised at great segments of the human race. . . . Whether the strong action of the American government has come in time remains to be seen . . . Men are becoming desperate. Fear of the future is in everyone's hearts [2]

END NOTES

1. JFK in History: Cuban Missile Crisis, John. F. Kennedy Presidential Library & Museum, http://www.jfklibrary.org/Historical+Resources/JFK+in+History/Cuban+Missile+Crisis.htm

2. Angela M. Lahr, *Millennial Dreams and Apocalyptic Nightmares*. (New York: Oxford University Press, 2007), 116–17.

November 22, 1963

The Assassination of John F. Kennedy

PRESIDENT KENNEDY was thinking ahead to his bid for re-election when he decided to take a trip to Texas in the fall of 1963. There was support to be drummed up for the Kennedy-Johnson ticket as well as local candidates, and political fence mending to achieve among feuding Democratic Party leaders. JFK left for the Lone Star State on Thursday, November 21, along with his wife, Jacqueline, who was just beginning to resume official duties after the loss of their infant son in August. The couple visited San Antonio and the space center in Houston, then they left for Dallas the following morning after an official breakfast at the Fort Worth Chamber of Commerce. At the airport they boarded a motorcade that would travel through downtown Dallas on its way to an appearance at the Trade Mart.

Kennedy rode in the back seat of the open Lincoln Continental with Mrs. Kennedy, and in the front were Texas Governor John Connally and his wife, Nellie. Mrs. Connally took note of the admiring crowd lined up on both sides of the route, turned to Kennedy and said, "Mr. President, you can't say Dallas doesn't love you." A heartbeat later as they passed the Texas School Book Depository, shots rang out, hitting both Kennedy and Connally. The First Lady sprang from her seat across the back of the limousine where Secret Service Agent Clint Hill intercepted her as the Lincoln sped off to Parkland Memorial Hospital. By the time doctors began working on Kennedy, it was far too late to save him from a gaping head wound. He was pronounced dead at 1 PM, CST. (Connally survived.)

As word spread of the assassination, Americans went into deep shock, hardly able to absorb that their leader was dead and that Lyndon Johnson, sworn into office aboard Air Force One, had taken his place. Due to the intense coverage of the assassination, its aftermath, and the funeral with its dramatic procession to Arlington National Cemetery, there was "a concert of grief such as human technology could never before have made possible."[1]

John W. McCormack, Speaker of the House, commented on Kennedy's place in history:

Now that our great leader has been taken from us in a cruel death, we are bound to feel shattered and helpless in the face of our loss. This is but natural, but as the first bitter pangs of our incredulous grief begin to pass we must thank God that we were privileged, however briefly, to have had this great man for our President. For he has now taken his place among the great figures of world history.

While this is an occasion of deep sorrow it should be also one of dedication. We must have the determination to unite and carry on the spirit of John Fitzgerald Kennedy for a strengthened America and a future world of peace.[2]

Historian William Manchester said that life return to normal after the official thirty days of mourning ended for the nation, when the flags were returned to the tops of poles, and business as usual ensued. He noted, instead, that expressions of grief continued for quite some time, including a candlelight vigil for the President along Fifth Avenue in New York where about a thousand people participated, those he referred to as "sheep without a shepherd."[3]

END NOTES

1. Sydney E. Ahlstrom, *A Religious History of the American People*, vol. 1 (Garden City, NY: Image Books, 1975), 1079, 1083.

2. Eulogy at the Capitol Rotunda, November 24, 1963, John F. Kennedy Presidential Library and Museum, http://www.jfklibrary.org/Historical+Resources/Archives/Reference+Desk/Eulogies+to+the+Late+President+Kennedy.htm.

3. William Manchester, *One Brief Shining Moment*. (Boston: Little, Brown and Company, 1983), 270–71.

January 1968

The Tet Offensive

IN THE MID-1960s America found itself enmeshed in a war in Southeast Asia that began as an effort to save the people of South Vietnam from being consumed by communism. The small nation had been under Chinese control for a thousand years before the French gradually made it into one of its colonies in the late nineteenth century. After World War II, French rule was threatened by the communist Viet Minh, who fought to attain independence under Ho Chi Minh, with support from the Soviet Union. France relented in 1954, and what eventually happened was a division of the country into the communist north and a southern republic—first under Bao Dai, then Ngo Dinh Diem. When the north went after Diem's regime, the U.S. began sending military advisors and armaments to support South Vietnam to prevent a "domino effect" in Southeast Asia of one country after another falling under communist control. By 1968, a half million Americans were fighting in Vietnam; eventually over 58,000 would die in the struggle with some 350,000 casualties.

In late January, 1968 as the Vietnamese prepared to celebrate their (lunar) new year, Ho Chi Minh launched a massive offensive involving some 80,000 troops against the south and its American allies, who were initially stunned by the show of power. They rallied to contain the attacks, and the North's campaign ended by September of the same year. U.S. involvement in the war continued until President Nixon's administration ended it with the Paris Peace Accords in January 1973; the South fell to the North Vietnamese two years later.

At the time of the Tet Offensive, U.S. Naval aviator John McCain was languishing in a Hanoi prison, having been shot down over that city the year before. He would remain a POW until his release in 1973, enduring ongoing beatings, interrogations, and inhumane deprivation.

During one cross-examination, McCain's questioner decided to ask him about American religious traditions asking, "What is Easter?"

"I told him," McCain said, "that it was the time of year we celebrated the death and resurrection of the Son of God. As I recounted the events of Christ's passion, His crucifixion, death, resurrection, and assumption to heaven, I saw my curious interrogator furrow his brow in disbelief."

The young man asked, "You say he died?"

McCain answered that yes, Jesus died.

"Three days, He was dead?" came the next question.

"Yes," the American answered. "Then he came alive again. People saw Him and then He went back to heaven." The interrogator stared at him for a few moments, left the room, then came back looking angry.

"'Mac Kane, the officer says you tell nothing but lies. Go back to your room,' he ordered. The mystery of my faith proving incomprehensible to him."[1]

END NOTES

1. John McCain, *Faith of My Fathers*. (New York: Random House, 1999), 223.

April 4 and June 5, 1968

The Assassinations of Martin Luther King, Jr. and Robert F. Kennedy

FOLLOWING THE 1956 Montgomery bus boycott, the Rev. Dr. Martin Luther King, Jr. became a nationally respected leader of the civil rights movement. He encouraged blacks to pursue nonviolent means in their pursuit for equality on all levels of American society, and he led peaceful protest marches in Selma, Alabama and Washington, D.C. In the latter event in August, 1963, he gave one of the most recognized and inspiring addresses in U.S. history, known as the "I Have a Dream Speech," delivered before roughly a quarter of a million people. It was there that he proclaimed:

> I have a dream that my four little children will one day live in a nation where they will not be judged by the

color of their skin, but by the content of their character. . . .

Now is the time to lift our nation from the quick-
sand of racial injustice to the solid rock of brother-
hood. Now is the time to make justice a reality for all
of God's children. Let freedom ring. And when this
happens, and when we allow freedom to ring—when
we let it ring from every village and every hamlet, from
every state and every city, we will be able to speed up
that day when all of God's children—black men and
white men, Jews and Gentiles, Protestants and
Catholics—will be able to join hands and sing in the
words of the old Negro spiritual: "Free at last! Free at
last! Thank God Almighty, we are free at last!"[1]

In 1964 King was awarded the Nobel Peace Prize for his
efforts, labors that often enveloped him in controversy and
put himself and his family in danger from those who passionately opposed his work. On April 3, 1968, a bomb threat
delayed his flight to Memphis, where he was going to support
striking sanitation workers. King gave a speech that night
laced with prophetic insight, considering what happened the
following day. He told a packed church audience:

And then I got to Memphis. And some began to say
the threats, or talk about the threats that were out
(sic). What would happen to me from some of our
sick white brothers? Well, I don't know what will

happen now. We've got some difficult days ahead. But it doesn't matter with me now. Because I've been to the mountaintop. And I don't mind. Like anybody, I would like to live a long life. Longevity has its place. But I'm not concerned about that now. I just want to do God's will. And He's allowed me to go up to the mountain. And I've looked over. And I've seen the promised land. I may not get there with you. But I want you to know tonight, that we, as a people, will get to the promised land. So I'm happy, tonight. I'm not worried about anything. I'm not fearing any man. Mine eyes have seen the glory of the coming of the Lord. [2]

In the early evening of April 4 on the balcony of his motel in Memphis, King was shot as he talked with aides. He died roughly an hour later after emergency surgery.

New York Senator Robert F. Kennedy was running for President at the time of the assassination, and he spoke of its impact on a personal level, having lost his older brother to such a murder five years earlier. He encouraged the nation to pray through the difficult time in which they found themselves:

My favorite poet was Aeschylus. He wrote: "In our sleep, pain which cannot forget falls drop by drop upon the heart until, in our own despair, against our will, comes wisdom through the awful grace of God."

What we need in the United States is not division; what we need in the United States is not hatred; what we need in the United States is not violence or law-lessness; but love and wisdom, and compassion toward one another, and a feeling of justice toward those who still suffer within our country, whether they be white or they be black.

So I shall ask you tonight to return home, to say a prayer for the family of Martin Luther King, that's true, but more importantly to say a prayer for our own country, which all of us love—a prayer for understanding and that compassion of which I spoke.[3]

The following day, Kennedy addressed a group in Cleveland where he told them:

It is not the concern of any one race. The victims of the violence are black and white, rich and poor, young and old, famous and unknown. They are, most important of all, human beings whom other human beings loved and needed. No one— no matter where he lives or what he does—can be certain who will suffer from some senseless act of bloodshed. And yet it goes on and on and on in this country of ours.[4]

Kennedy was engaged in a tight contest for the Democratic nomination with fellow senator Eugene McCarthy of Minnesota. When the polls closed in the crucial California primary on June 4 and the ballots were counted, Kennedy bested his opponent. Just after midnight he went to the ballroom of the Ambassador Hotel in Los Angeles to address his supporters, giving a brief, upbeat speech. In order to get through the crowd more quickly, he then took a short cut through the hotel's kitchen where an assassin fired three shots into Kennedy, including a fatal head wound. Surgery was unable to save his life, and the senator died early on the morning of June 6.

When Martin Luther King gave his final speech, he quoted the words of *The Battle Hymn of the Republic,* and in a moving portion of RFK's funeral at St. Patrick's Cathedral in New York, entertainer Andy Williams sang that same song. It carried a poignant reminder that while national leaders rise and fall, God remains firmly at the helm:

> In the beauty of the lilies Christ was born across the sea,
> With a glory in His bosom that transfigures you and me:
> As He died to make men holy, let us die to make men
>   free,
> While God in marching on.
> Glory, glory, hallelujah!
> Glory, glory, hallelujah!
> While God is marching on![5]

END NOTES

1. American Rhetoric, Top 100 Speeches, Martin Luther King, Jr., "I Have a Dream," http://www.americanrhetoric.com/speeches/mlkihaveadream.htm

2. Ibid., "I've Been to the Mountaintop," http://www.americanrhetoric.com/speeches/mlkivebeentothemountaintop.htm

3. Robert F. Kennedy, "Statement on the Assassination of Martin Luther King, Jr.," Indianapolis, Indiana, April 4, 1968, Robert F. Kennedy Memorial, http://www.rfkmemorial.org/lifevision/assassinationofmartinlutherkingjr/

4. Ibid., "On the Mindless Menace of Violence," City Club of Cleveland, April 5, 1968, Robert F. Kennedy Memorial Foundation, http://www.rfkmemorial.org/lifevision/onthemindless menaceofviolence/

5. "The Battle Hymn of the Republic," Julia Ward Howe, 1861.

July 20, 1969

The First Man Walks on the Moon

IN A SPEECH at Rice University in Texas on September 12, 1962, President John F. Kennedy issued a bold challenge to get America on the moon by the end of the 1960s. He told his audience:

> We choose to go to the moon. We choose to go to the moon in this decade and do the other things, not because they are easy, but because they are hard, because that goal will serve to organize and measure the best of our energies and skills, because that challenge is one that we are willing to accept, one we are unwilling to postpone, and one which we intend to win, and the others, too.
>
> It is for these reasons that I regard the decision last year to shift our efforts in space from low to high

gear as among the most important decisions that will
be made during my incumbency in the office of the
Presidency.[1]

Throughout that period, manned space flight progressed
from putting men in orbit via the Mercury program to the
more complicated Gemini flights when an American man
first walked in space. It was, however, the Apollo spacecraft
that would ultimately reach the moon, a goal that appeared
to be well within reach at Christmas time in 1968 when
Frank Borman, James Lovell, and William Anders circum-
navigated the moon ten times aboard the Apollo 8. On
Christmas Eve, they transmitted astounding photos of the
earth from the moon to the world some quarter of a million
miles away, images that continue to inspire. Anders told the
people of Earth that he and his crew had a message for them,
and he began to read the Creation story from Genesis 1:1–4.

Less than a year later, on July 20, 1969, the first human
being set his foot on the moon. When he stepped off the lad-
der of the lunar module, Neil Armstrong uttered the historic
words, "That's one small step for a man, one giant leap for
mankind." During the next three years, a dozen more men
would follow in Armstrong's tracks, including James Irwin,
who traveled there in April 1971 along with David R. Scott.
The experience had a profound impact on Irwin who, having
felt God's power as never before, became an ardent believer
in Jesus Christ. He decided at that time to spend the rest of
his life telling the world he had seen from so high above about

the One who had come to save it. He once told a journalist,

> While on the moon, at the end of the first day explor-
> ing the rugged lunar highlands, I was reminded of my
> favorite Biblical passage from Psalms. While speaking
> by radio to Mission Control in Houston, I began
> quoting the passage, 'I'll look into the hills from
> whence cometh my help,' and then I added quickly,
> 'but, of course, we get quite a bit of help from Hous-
> ton, too. [2]

He concluded, "It is more significant that God walked on earth than that man walked on the moon. . . . .my own life is given purpose and perspective through God who walks on this earth in Jesus. In that sense we are a visited planet!"[3]

END NOTES

1. John F. Kennedy, "Address at Rice University on the Nation's Space Effort," September 12, 1962, John F. Kennedy Presidential Library & Museum, http://www.jfklibrary.org/Historical+ Resources/Archives/Reference+Desk/Speeches/JFK/003POF03 SpaceEffort09121962.htm

2. Dan Wooding, "He Landed on the Moon But Couldn't Work a British Pay Phone," Christian-Connection, http://www. christian-connection.org/article.php?sid=411

3. Ibid.

May 1970

The Shootings at Kent State University

WHEN AMERICAN involvement began in the Vietnam War, most of the country was behind the military action, including the majority of college students. That began to change, however, due to the poor political execution of the conflict largely caused by fear that the Communist Chinese would expand the war if the United States showed the full extent of its might against North Vietnam. As a result, there were unnecessarily heavy American losses and no end in sight. In addition, the inception of a draft led to a frenzy of anti-war protests on many college campuses, which included sit-ins at administration buildings, the burning of draft cards, and intense confrontations with the police and National Guard. By the end of the 1960s, such demonstrations were commonplace at schools like Columbia University and Berkeley, but when a protest resulted in the deaths of students at a heart-land college, Americans were shocked.

At the end of April, President Nixon had announced that the U.S. military would be moving into Cambodia, which had been supplying the communist North Vietnamese. Pre-dictably, students who wanted the war to end right away dis-agreed with the decision and turned out against it in large numbers, including in Ohio where, for several days, young people fought the police and caused property damage. On Monday, May 4, at Kent State University, the Ohio National Guard fired into a group of protestors after they began throwing stones at the soldiers. Four students died, and eleven others were wounded. Of those who perished, two were simply walking on their way to classes.[1]

Many Americans wondered what the current generation of young people was coming to, yet there was still a great deal of hope as evidenced by a historic revival that same spring. The entire student body of Asbury College in Wilmore, Kentucky had turned out for 10 a.m. chapel on a cold February day.[2] The dean had been scheduled to preach that morning, but at the last minute he decided to share what God had been doing in his life and offered students an opportunity to do the same. A few stepped to the platform to give their testimonies, and as they did so, a tremendous sense of God's presence enveloped Hughes Auditorium. When the hour ended, one professor invited anyone who wanted to come forward to the altar. As the hymn, *Just As I Am*, played, a large group of students swarmed around the rail, ignoring the bell that signaled the resumption of classes. Public confession of sin ensued, fractured relationships were healed, and people forgot about eating, drinking, sleeping or anything but declarations of guilt and praises of joy for forgiveness in Christ. The administration cancelled the rest of the day's classes as the auditorium remained jammed with students, faculty, and their spouses, then expanded to include people from the seminary across the street as well as the entire community.

The revival spread wherever Asbury students traveled to tell people what God was doing on their small campus. It lasted fully one week, then lingered for the rest of the semester as people continued to experience God's special movement and grace. One Asburian reported what was happening at school to her hometown newspaper in Michigan:

> There is a new kind of demonstration at Asbury during these days of national college sit-ins—not in the administration offices, but in the college and seminary chapels. Students are throwing around a lot of three, four, and five-letter words, too. Words like "joy," "love," "pray," and "faith." They plan to turn the world upside down, not because they're troublemakers, but for the sake of Jesus Christ![3]

Similarly, one reporter, who was tired of covering student riots, rejoiced in what was happening down in Kentucky. He wrote, "If those kids run out of something to pray for about 2 o'clock in the morning, ask them to pray for me."[4]

END NOTES

1. Rebecca Price Janney, *Great Stories in American History*, 170.
2. Ibid., 171–177.
3. Ibid., 174.
4. Ibid., 174–75.

1972

Détente: President Nixon in Russia and China

A S A YOUNG Congressman in the post-World War II era, Richard Nixon developed a reputation as a strong leader in the fight against communist infiltration of the United States government and society while serving on the House Un-American Activities Committee. He went on to become a Senator from California and Vice President under Dwight D. Eisenhower during which time he engaged in a famous "kitchen debate" with Premier Khrushchev of the Soviet Union, sparring with him about the superiority of democracy over communism. John F. Kennedy defeated the Cold Warrior for the Presidency in the 1960 election, but Nixon maintained an active political profile.

In the late 1960s he surprised some people by suggesting that it was unwise for the United States to shun completely the Chinese communists. He stated, " . . . we simply cannot afford to leave China forever outside the family of nations, there to nurture its fantasies, cherish its hates, and threaten its neighbors."[1] It isn't a stretch to conclude that he felt similarly about the antagonistic relationship the U.S. had with the other communist superpower, Russia.

After Nixon became President of the United States in January 1969, he quickly began signaling both Russia and China that he wanted to open diplomatic relations. In February 1972 he made a historic visit to the Far East where he held talks with Chinese leaders, the first U.S. President to go to that country. That May, he traveled once again into communist territory to meet with Premier Brezhnev in Moscow, and the two leaders signed the Strategic Arms Limitations Treaty. Although far from conclusive in its sweep, it was a first big step back from the nuclear brink. Gradually, the three nations began to pursue cultural, diplomatic, and economic ties with each other.

Someone else who had been desirous of a more open relationship with the communists, the Russians in particular, was evangelist Billy Graham. As he began to take his crusades across the world in the 1950s, he felt a tug on his spirit to one day preach the gospel message inside the Soviet Union, although at the time, it seemed utterly impossible. Shortly after President Nixon went to Moscow, Graham's team started talking to Soviet officials about allowing him to come behind the Iron Curtain. They permitted him to go to Hungary and Poland, and Graham continued to pray for an opening to Russia itself, which happened in 1982. It wasn't, however, until ten years later that he held a full-blown evangelistic crusade in Moscow, an event that bore much fruit for the kingdom. In three days, Russians packed the stadium to capacity and beyond—35,000 to 50,000 per meeting—with nearly 43,000 of them signing "commitment cards" proclaiming that they wanted to be followers of the Lord whom their leaders had been denying since 1917.[2]

END NOTES

1. "Nixon's China Game," The American Experience, http://www.pbs.org/wgbh/amex/china/peopleevents/pande01.html

2. "Billy: a Personal Look at Billy Graham," Sherwood Elliot Wirt, http://www.ccel.us/billy.ch26.html

August 9, 1974

Richard Nixon Resigns as President

FRESH FROM his foreign policy triumphs in China and Russia and with a promise to end American involvement in the Vietnam War honorably, Richard Nixon won in a landslide over Democrat George McGovern in the 1972 election, taking all but one state and the District of Columbia. Voters trusted him when he dismissed a break-in at the Democratic Party headquarters at the Watergate Complex by assuring them, "I can say categorically that no one on the White House staff, no one in this administration presently employed, was involved in this very bizarre incident."[1]

Following the election and his second inauguration, however, an investigation into the burglary began to inch its way closer to some of the President's closest men, including Attorney General John Mitchell, and White House lawyers

Charles Colson and John Dean—who accused Nixon of being involved in a cover-up of the incident—and the director of the Committee to Re-Elect the President, Jeb Stuart Magruder.

In May 1974, the House of Representatives began impeachment hearings against Nixon, and by August it became clear to the public that the President had indeed been mixed up in several offenses related to the Watergate conspiracy. He went before the nation on August 8, 1974 on television to announce that he would be resigning from the Presidency the next day and that Vice President Gerald R. Ford would be taking the oath of office. He had not been Nixon's running mate in either the 1968 or 1972 elections; rather, he had taken the place of Vice President Spiro T. Agnew in 1973 after Agnew resigned while facing charges of tax evasion, bribery, and money laundering while he was Maryland's governor. According to the terms of the twenty-fifth Amendment to the Constitution, House Minority Leader Ford stepped into the void.

When Ford became President, he was painfully aware that he had not been the direct choice of the American people to be their leader. In his address to the nation after assuming office, he recognized this openly and asked for prayer because he was going to need God's help in the difficult days ahead:

> The oath that I have taken is the same oath that was taken by George Washington and by every President under the Constitution. But I assume the Presidency

under extraordinary circumstances never before experienced by Americans. This is an hour of history that troubles our minds and hurts our hearts.

Therefore, I feel it is my first duty to make an unprecedented compact with my countrymen. Not an inaugural address, not a fireside chat, not a campaign speech—just a little straight talk among friends. And I intend it to be the first of many.

I am acutely aware that you have not elected me as your President by your ballots, and so I ask you to confirm me as your President with your prayers. And I hope that such prayers will also be the first of many. . .

My fellow Americans, our long national nightmare is over.

Our Constitution works; our great Republic is a government of laws and not of men. Here the people rule. But there is a higher Power, by whatever name we honor Him, who ordains not only righteousness but love, not only justice but mercy.

As we bind up the internal wounds of Watergate, more painful and more poisonous than those of foreign wars, let us restore the golden rule to our political process, and let brotherly love purge our hearts of suspicion and of hate.

In the beginning, I asked you to pray for me. Before closing, I ask again your prayers, for Richard Nixon and for his family. May our former President, who brought peace to millions, find it for himself.

May God bless and comfort his wonderful wife and daughters, whose love and loyalty will forever be a shining legacy to all who bear the lonely burdens of the White House.

I can only guess at those burdens, although I have witnessed at close hand the tragedies that befell three Presidents and the lesser trials of others.

With all the strength and all the good sense I have gained from life, with all the confidence my family, my friends, and my dedicated staff impart to me, and with the good will of countless Americans I have encountered in recent visits to 40 States, I now solemnly reaffirm my promise I made to you last December 6: to uphold the Constitution, to do what is right as God gives me to see the right, and to do the very best I can for America.

God helping me, I will not let you down.

Thank you.[2]

END NOTES

1. John A. Garraty, 911.
2. "Gerald R. Ford's Remarks on Taking the Oath of Office as President," August 4, 1974, Gerald R. Ford Presidential Library and Museum, http://www.ford.utexas.edu/

37

November 4, 1979–
January 20, 1981

The Iranian Hostage Crisis

AMERICA WENT into a slump in the period following Watergate when confidence in its leaders, as well as its power and position in the world, declined. In 1975 South Vietnam fell to the communist North Vietnamese, and Americans remaining in the country scrambled to get out safely, creating a humiliating image in the media. It was also a time of inflation and an energy crisis that resulted in cold houses and long lines at gas pumps. In 1979, a movie about a nuclear meltdown was released less than two weeks before an actual nuclear accident at Three Mile Island in Pennsylvania. It seemed that America had reached the limits of its once-exalted position in the world, a feeling that deepened in the fall when the Shah of Iran, a friend of the U.S., was deposed by the Islamic cleric Ayatollah

Ruhollah Khomeini. He was a fanatic who called America "the great Satan."

On November 4 a band of his followers seized the U.S. Embassy, taking more than sixty Americans hostage and demanding that the Shah be returned to Iran and America apologize for supporting him. If those terms were not met, the radicals threatened to try the hostages as spies and kill them. President Carter refused to give in to their conditions, and a long stalemate ensued. The ordeal captivated the nation for next 444 days, with Americans full of anger and worry over the fate of the captives, as well as our global reputation.

A few days after the seizure of the embassy, ABC News began running a late-night program that featured a daily update of the situation, eventually calling it "Nightline." It enjoyed great popularity, and its display of the days of captivity became a national slogan—"American Held Hostage: Day 15," and so on for the duration.

In April 1980, President Carter prepared a military rescue of the hostages that ended in a fiasco with two helicopters having to turn back due to technical problems and a dust storm. Another crashed in the desert killing eight people. Carter's failure in the crisis led to his sound defeat in the November elections to Republican Ronald Reagan. On the day of the latter's inauguration, January 20, 1981, the Iranians released the prisoners moments after he was sworn in as President. A cartoon of the day showed them looking up at a swarm of American military aircraft and saying, "Reagan must have been elected."

The former actor and California governor injected hope into America again, something he spoke of passionately in his inaugural address. He was a man of deep faith in God and in the greatness of America's national mission, someone who believed that the country could yet be a shining city on a hill and that its best days were still ahead. That day he said:

We have every right to dream heroic dreams. Those who say that we're in a time when there are no heroes, they just don't know where to look. You can see heroes every day going in and out of factory gates. Others, a handful in number, produce enough food to feed all of us and then the world beyond. You meet heroes across a counter, and they're on both sides of that counter. There are entrepreneurs with faith in themselves and faith in an idea who create new jobs, new wealth and opportunity. They're individuals and families whose taxes support the government and whose voluntary gifts support church, charity, culture, art, and education. Their patriotism is quiet, but deep. Their values sustain our national life. . .

Can we solve the problems confronting us? Well, the answer is an unequivocal and emphatic "yes." To paraphrase Winston Churchill, I did not take the oath I've just taken with the intention of presiding over the dissolution of the world's strongest economy. . .

Well, I believe we, the Americans of today, are ready to act worthy of ourselves, ready to do what must be done to ensure happiness and liberty for ourselves, our children, and our children's children. And as we renew ourselves here in our own land, we will be seen as having greater strength throughout the world. We will again be the exemplar of freedom and a beacon of hope for those who do not now have freedom...

I'm told that tens of thousands of prayer meetings are being held on this day, and for that I'm deeply grateful. We are a nation under God, and I believe God intended for us to be free. It would be fitting and good, I think, if on each Inaugural Day in future years it should be declared a day of prayer.[1]

END NOTES

1. Ronald Reagan's First Inaugural Address, January 20, 1981, Ronald Reagan Presidential Library, http://www.reagan.utexas .edu/archives/speeches/publicpapers.html

January 28, 1986

The Challenger Disaster

THE LAST MAN walked on the moon in December 1972, and afterwards the National Aeronautics and Space Administration went forward with a plan to develop a space shuttle for missions with scientific, military, and economic uses. In the spring of 1981, NASA launched *Columbia*, followed by *Challenger, Discovery, Atlantis,* and *Endeavor.* It didn't take long for the public to regard these undertakings as routine and commonplace rather than the thrilling adventures of the earlier space program.

There was, however, great interest in the *Challenger* space flight in late January, 1986 because it would be carrying the first teacher beyond earth's atmosphere. Christa McAuliffe was a social studies instructor at Concord High School in New Hampshire, and she would be using the space shuttle as her classroom for a series of lectures to be beamed down to

American schools. The public became fascinated with the personable teacher, who had been selected from more than 11,000 candidates.

Challenger was supposed to have flown several days earlier but was delayed by the prior shuttle's mission and bad weather. Finally, on the morning of January 28, the crew boarded the shuttle and blasted off at 11:38 on an unusually cold day for central Florida. With a large crowd in attendance and thousands of children watching on classroom televisions, *Challenger* ascended into the clear blue sky. Problems quickly developed, however, with an "O" ring that had not sealed properly in the cold, and when an enormous wind sheer slammed into the spacecraft, a plume developed that ruptured one of the external fuel tanks. Seventy-three seconds into the launch, *Challenger* exploded into a huge fireball that killed all seven astronauts and sent shock waves through the nation. People at the space center and watching on TV waited for someone from NASA to say something reassuring, that maybe they hadn't really seen what they thought they had. What came across the nation's airwaves, however, was a stunned, "Obviously a major malfunction. We have no downlink." This was followed by confirmation of the accident. "We have a report from the Flight Dynamics Officer that the vehicle has exploded."[1]

At the time of the accident, President Reagan was preparing for his State of the Union Address to be given later that evening. Instead, he postponed it and went on TV at 5 p.m. to speak to the public about the disaster. He told them:

We mourn seven heroes: Michael Smith, Dick Scobee, Judith Resnik, Ronald McNair, Ellison Onizuka, Gregory Jarvis, and Christa McAuliffe. We mourn their loss as a nation together.

For the families of the seven, we cannot bear, as you do, the full impact of this tragedy. But we feel the loss, and we're thinking about you so very much. Your loved ones were daring and brave, and they had that special grace, that special spirit that says, "Give me a challenge, and I'll meet it with joy." They had a hunger to explore the universe and discover its truths. They wished to serve, and they did. They served all of us. We've grown used to wonders in this century. It's hard to dazzle us. But for 25 years the United States space program has been doing just that. We've grown used to the idea of space, and perhaps we forget that we've only just begun. We're still pioneers. They, the members of the Challenger crew, were pioneers.

And I want to say something to the schoolchildren of America who were watching the live coverage of the shuttle's takeoff. I know it is hard to understand, but sometimes painful things like this happen. It's all part of the process of exploration and discovery. It's all part of taking a chance and expanding man's horizons. The future doesn't belong to the fainthearted; it belongs to the brave. The Challenger crew was pulling us into the future, and we'll continue to follow them . . .

There's a coincidence today. On this day 390 years ago, the great explorer Sir Francis Drake died aboard ship off the coast of Panama. In his lifetime the great frontiers were the oceans, and an historian later said, "He lived by the sea, died on it, and was buried in it." Well, today we can say of the Challenger crew: Their dedication was, like Drake's, complete.

The crew of the space shuttle Challenger honored us by the manner in which they lived their lives. We will never forget them, nor the last time we saw them, this morning, as they prepared for their journey and waved goodbye and "slipped the surly bonds of earth" to "touch the face of God."[2]

END NOTES

1. "Space Shuttle Challenger Disaster," Wikipedia, *The Free Encyclopedia*. October 26, 2008, http://en.wikipedia.org/wiki/Space_Shuttle_Challenger_disaster

2. "Address to the Nation on the Explosion of the Space Shuttle Challenger, January 28, 1986, Ronald Reagan Presidential Library Foundation, http://www.reaganlibrary.com/welcome.asp

1989

The Fall of Soviet Communism

DIPLOMATS told him to play it safe. The National Security Council and State Department considered the challenge naïve, that it would give Eastern Europeans false hope. Some cabinet officials said the message would offend Soviet Premier Gorbachev. Reagan had spent most of his public career speaking out against Soviet communism, and although Mikhail Gorbachev had introduced some reforms, the President remained skeptical. He knew these changes wouldn't be enough to set free the oppressed peoples of Russia or communist-controlled Eastern Europe. In the end, Reagan's principles motivated him to say what was on his heart. He told an aide that he was going to deliver the line that bothered many envoys. "The boys at State are going to kill me," he said, "but it's the right thing to do."[1]

Two major themes of his presidency had strong connections to his Christian faith. For years in his speeches he had envisioned America as a "shining city on a hill," a reference to Jesus' words in Matthew 5:14–15. Conversely, when the Soviet Union was formed in 1917, its leaders wanted to purge religion, particularly Christianity, from Russia and all the other nations it would come to dominate. According to former Premier Gorbachev, "our (communist) ideologues carried out a wholesale war on religion . . . Atheism took rather savage forms in our country at that time."[2] Because they believed Christianity hurt a person's allegiance to the state, Soviet despots impounded all buildings and land from Russian Orthodox Churches, required people to be married in civil ceremonies, and replaced baptisms and funerals with their own rituals. They turned churches into nightclubs and storage facilities. Officials required teachers to report any students and their parents or grandparents who attended religious services.

Ronald Reagan's second theme as President was to relegate the Soviet system to what he called "the ash heap of history."[3] On March 20, 1981, just two months after taking the oath of office, he told an audience, "Only by building . . . a wall of spiritual resolve, can we, as a free people, hope to protect our own heritage and make it someday the birthright of all men."[4]

Ten days later as he was leaving the Washington Hilton following a speech, a would-be assassin shot him. The President barely survived a gunshot wound to his left lung that would have killed him had it moved an inch in a different direction. During Reagan's recovery, he told his daughter Maureen that he believed God had spared his life for a reason. He wrote in his diary: "Whatever happens now, I owe my life to God and will try to serve him every way I can."[5] According to Edmund Morris, the President meant "among other things, a coming to terms with Evil. Not the . . . evil . . . of (would-be assassin) John Hinckley's assault, but that institutional murder of all liberties known as Soviet communism."[6]

President Reagan riled any number of people by an increasing aggressiveness toward the U.S.S.R.'s leadership. In a speech to the National Association of Evangelicals in Orlando on March 8, 1983, he came right out and called Russia "evil:"

> So, I urge you to speak out against those who would place the United States in a position of military and moral inferiority. You know, I've always believed that old Screwtape reserved his best efforts for those of you in the church. So, in your discussions of the nuclear freeze proposals, I urge you to beware the temptation of pride—the temptation of blithely declaring yourselves above it all and label both sides equally at fault, to ignore the facts of history and the aggressive impulses of an evil empire, to simply call the arms race a giant misunderstanding and thereby remove yourself from the struggle between right and wrong and good and evil.[7]

When Mikhail Gorbechev became Soviet Premier in March 1985, he said he wanted to reform (*perestroika*) the government, to make it more open (*glasnost*) to other ways of thought. Many Western officials believed he would improve conditions for the Russian people and ease up on Eastern Europe. However, Ronald Reagan wasn't going to trust him until he saw actual results. He wanted to see that people had more economic and religious freedom. On June 12, 1987, the President delivered a challenge to Gorbachev in West Berlin, near the Brandenburg Gate of the wall. Many believe that the address marked the beginning of the end of Soviet communism.

Prior to the speech as he met with his hosts, Reagan received a warning from a West German official to be careful about what he said; the East Germans had the ability to bug their meeting. Because Reagan wore a hearing aid, that made him even more vulnerable. That's all he needed to hear. He wrote of that incident, "Well, when I heard that, I went out to a landing that was even closer to the building and began sounding off about what I thought of a government that penned in its people like farm animals."[8]

A while later as he stood at the wall, President Reagan said it was "as stark a symbol as anyone could ever expect to see of the contrast between two different political systems: on one side, people held captive by a failed and corrupt totalitarian government, on the other, freedom, enterprise, prosperity."[9] Then he told the crowd:

In the 1950s, Khrushchev predicted: "We will bury you." But in the West today, we see a free world that has achieved a level of prosperity and well-being unprecedented in all human history. In the Communist world, we see failure, technological backwardness, declining standards of health, even want of the most basic kind— too little food. Even today, the Soviet Union still cannot feed itself. After these four decades, then, there stands before the entire world one great and inescapable conclusion: Freedom leads to prosperity. Freedom replaces the ancient hatreds among the nations with comity and peace. Freedom is the victor.

And now the Soviets themselves may, in a limited way, be coming to understand the importance of freedom. We hear much from Moscow about a new policy of reform and openness. Some political prisoners have been released. Certain foreign news broadcasts are no longer being jammed. Some economic enterprises have been permitted to operate with greater freedom from state control.

Are these the beginnings of profound changes in the Soviet state? Or are they token gestures, intended to raise false hopes in the West, or to strengthen the Soviet system without changing it? We welcome change and openness; for we believe that freedom and security go together, that the advance of human liberty can only strengthen the cause of world peace.

There is one sign the Soviets can make that would be unmistakable, that would advance dramatically the cause of freedom and peace.

General Secretary Gorbachev, if you seek peace, if you seek prosperity for the Soviet Union and Eastern Europe, if you seek liberalization: Come here to this gate! Mr. Gorbachev, open this gate! Mr. Gorbachev, tear down this wall![10]

While officials who wanted to appease Russia cringed, the people living under communism took heart. Reagan later wrote, "I never dreamed that in less than three years the wall would come down and a six-thousand-pound section of it would be sent to me for my presidential library."[11]

The Soviet system started unraveling in 1989, as pro-democracy forces ran far ahead of the reforms Gorbachev had envisioned. Between November 9 and 11, protestors tore down the hated Berlin Wall, and one by one, the Eastern Bloc countries declared independence from Soviet domination, led by many believers in Jesus Christ, particularly in Romania. On December 8, 1991, the Soviet Union was dissolved.

END NOTES

1. Peter Robinson". *How Ronald Reagan Changed My Life*. (New York: HarperCollins Publishers Inc., 2003), 103.

2. Paul Kengor. *God and Ronald Reagan*. (New York: Regan-Books, 2004), 60.

3. 1982 Speech before the British Parliament, Ronald Reagan:

The Heritage Foundation Remembers, http://www.reagans heritage.org/reagan/html/reagan_panel_pipes.shtml

4. Kengor, 87.

5. Ibid., 199.

6. Ibid., 200.

7. Remarks at the Annual Convention of the National Association of Evangelicals in Orlando, FL, March 8, 1983, The Ronald Reagan Presidential Library Foundation, http://www.reagan.utexas.edu/archives/speeches/1983/30883b.htm

8. Robinson, 681.

9. Ronald Reagan, *An American Life.* (New York: Simon and Schuster, 199), 680.

10. Remarks on East-West Relations at the Brandenburg Gate in West Berlin , June 12, 1987, The Ronald Reagan Presidential Library Foundation, http://www.reagan.utexas.edu/archives/speeches/1983/30883b.htm

11. Reagan, 683.

August 2, 1990–
February 28, 1991

The Persian Gulf War

IRAQ'S SADDAM Hussein, one of the world's most brutal dictators, launched an invasion of neighboring Kuwait on August 2, 1990 to build up an empire for his own glory. Because some of his top advisors opposed the military effort, fearing international consequences, Saddam had them executed, and Kuwait succumbed to Iraq's superior power. The United Nations reacted with economic sanctions against Iraq, while the U.S. and Great Britain began mobilizing a multinational force.

On August 7 President George H.W. Bush sent U.S. troops into Saudi Arabia to protect that nation from Iraqi advances in what became known as Operation Desert Shield. That November, the U.N. passed a resolution requiring that Iraq withdraw from Kuwait by January 15 or face a major battle against nearly one million soldiers from around the world, led principally by the United States. Saddam remained adamant, thumbing his nose at the rest of world that he promised to trounce in what he claimed would be "the mother of all battles."

A massive campaign against Iraq began on January 17, the first time in history that people were able to watch moment-by-moment media coverage of a war on TV. Americans watched in awe as our impressive technology was unleashed against Saddam's military, especially as "smart bombs" found particular targets with great precision and destructive power. And yet, a much different, even more dominant kind of force was at work during the six weeks of the conflict that ended in a decisive Iraqi defeat.

According to Colonel E.H. Jim Ammerman, a U.S. Army Chaplain who served in the Gulf, tens of thousands of American fighting men and women came to know Christ during the brief war, and others found a renewed faith.[1] "Saddam declared the war a 'holy' one, but the United States would be the nation to experience the revival,"[2] Ammerman said. "Even during the early days of deployment, some Bible studies were going on for as long as eight hours. There was a hunger like I had never experienced in any war I'd served in."[3] While the troops in the Middle East grappled with desert conditions and the uncertainties of combat, people on the home front were also turning to Christ in large numbers; church attendance rose dramatically across the nation during the conflict. Even those newspaper editors with a secular orientation encouraged readers to pray.[4]

When the war was over, President Bush issued a special Proclamation of thanksgiving on March 7, 1991:

> As the Psalmist wrote, "O give thanks to the Lord for he is gracious, for His mercy endures forever. . . ."
>
> Almighty God has answered the prayers of millions of people with the liberation of Kuwait and the end of offensive operations in the Persian Gulf region. As we prepare to welcome home our courageous service men and women and join in the joyful celebrations of the Kuwaiti people, it is fitting that we give thanks to our Heavenly Father, our help and shield, for His mercy and protection . . .
>
> We thank the Lord for His favor, and we are profoundly grateful for the relatively low number of allied casualties, a fact described by the commanding general as "miraculous."
>
> As the Psalmist wrote, "Come behold the works of the Lord . . . He makes wars to cease to the end of the earth."[5]

END NOTES

1. Colonel E.H. Jim Ammerman, *After the Storm*. (Nashville: StarSong Communications, 1991), xxv.
2. Ibid., 9.
3. Ibid., 96.
4. Ibid., 35.
5. Ibid., ix–x.

April 19, 1995

The Oklahoma City Bombing

UNTIL FEBRUARY 26, 1993, terrorism was something that happened to people in other countries, not to Americans. Most people shook their heads, and sometimes their fists, and felt thankful for the safety that Americans enjoyed from such perils when they heard of horrific suicide bombings in Israel, or Libyan hijackings against defenseless civilians. On that winter morning, however, a car bomb planted by a group of Muslim extremists shattered the garage under the first tower of New York's World Trade Center, killing six and injuring more than 1,000 people. The circle of safety from terrorism had been broken. Two years later, it would happen again, under different circumstances.

At just after 9 a.m. on April 19, 1995, a Ryder Truck that was parked in front of the federal building in Oklahoma City exploded, sheering off a third of the edifice, killing 168 people, wounding over 800, and causing destruction in over 300 buildings. The blast was felt up to ten miles away. This time, however, the terrorists who planned and executed the attack were homegrown, militants bent on lashing out at the government that had carried out armed strikes against the radical Branch Davidians in Waco, Texas and the Ruby Ridge compound in Idaho. Timothy McVeigh and Terry Nichols carried out their assault on the Alfred P. Murrah Federal Building on the second anniversary of the Waco siege, shattering many lives. In spite of the tragic scope of the event, attorney Bob Johnson, who served as the chairman of the Oklahoma City National Memorial Trust, said those who lived through the bombing had a message to send to the world: "evil did not triumph here."[1]

One of the survivors was Patti Hall, who worked for the Federal Employees Credit Union at the time of the assault; her legs were crushed, her lung punctured, and her collarbone broken as a result of the explosion. In addition, she endured sixteen surgeries and a five-day coma that doctors induced so she wouldn't have to remember the trauma of the operations.[2] She told a reporter that what got her through the nightmare was her faith in God.

Like her, Jannie Coverdale leaned on God to get her through the pain of her terrible losses. A grandmother raising her two grandsons, she was working at the tax assessor's office inside the federal building while her boys stayed at the day care center. Their bodies were discovered four days after the bombing. Coverdale's initial response was to rail at God and tell him that she would never serve him again for allowing such a thing to happen.[3] Six months after the attack, however, she moved to a different apartment building and met a little boy named Adrian, a seven year-old who lived with his mother and with whom Coverdale developed an especially tight bond; she eventually became Adrian's legal guardian. She said that while he helped bring her back to life, it was also thoughts of her dead two year-old grandson, Elijah that brought her back to God. "One night," she said, "I had just crawled into bed. I heard Elijah say, 'Say your prayers, Granny. Say your prayers.'" [4] And she did.

END NOTES

1. "Evil Did Not Triumph," by Terry Horne, Staff Writer, April 15, 2001, *The Indianapolis Star*, http://www2.indystar.com/library/factfiles/crime/national/1995/oklahoma_city_bombing/stories/2001_0415.html

2. "Survivors to McVeigh: Why?" by Terry Horne, Staff Writer, February 4, 2001, *The Indianapolis Star*, http://www2.indystar.com/library/factfiles/crime/national/1995/oklahoma_city_bombing/stories/2001_0204.html

3. Horne, April 15, 2001.

4. Ibid.

September 11, 2001

The Terrorist Attacks on America

That Tuesday morning dazzled like a brilliant jewel in late summer, the skies clear and blue over New York City and Washington, D.C. Workers bustling to their jobs and children on school buses went about their routines completely unaware that a storm more devastating than a catgeory five hurricane or a ruinous tornado loomed in the cobalt blue heavens. At 8:46 a.m. American Airlines Flight 11 out of Boston veered off its path to Los Angeles and headed towards Manhattan where five hijackers connected to the terrorist group Al-Qaeda crashed into the North Tower of the World Trade Center. It exploded into a fireball, killing seventy-six passengers and eleven crew members as it also began burning away the structural supports of one of the world's largest skyscrapers.

Firefighters, paramedics, police and other rescue personnel rushed to the sight while bystanders watched in horror as flames consumed the top part of the building, causing some who were trapped inside to jump. President Bush learned of the incident just before addressing a group of students in Sarasota, Florida; he and his advisors initially thought that the crash might be a tragic accident. No one could have imagined the terror about to be unleashed on the nation.

Seventeen minutes after Flight 11 rammed into the North Tower, New Yorkers, along with countless Americans watching on television, witnessed United Airlines 175 slam into the South Tower, setting it on fire and killing sixty-five people on the plane. White House Chief of Staff Andrew Card approached President Bush and whispered the news. The Commander in Chief's face went wintry. It was clear that this was a coordinated attack by enemies of America, and no one except the Islamic militants knew what might happen next. A little over a half hour later at 9:37, a packed Washington to Los Angeles flight abruptly changed direction and ran into the Pentagon, killing 189 people on board and 125 on the ground. Chaos ensued in both New York and Washington as events spun out of control. Office workers and eyewitnesss scrambled to assist the trapped and injured as well as to flee for their own safety while professional rescuers hurried against time to rescue as many as possible.

At 9:59 the South Tower of the World Trade Center fell in a storm of dust and fragments, taking many lives with it. Minutes later at 10:03, United Airlines Flight 93 crashed into a field in Shanksville, Pennsylvania. The forty passengers and crew had discovered from friends and loved ones on their cell phones what was happening in New York and Washington, and when four hijackers seized control of their aircraft, many on the plane decided to do their best to thwart their evil intentions—to destroy either the Capitol building or the White House. They decided not to allow this to happen, to the best of their ability. Passenger Tom Burnett told his wife, "Don't worry, we're going to do something."[1]

Another passenger, Todd Beamer, ended up speaking to an operator while trying to contact his wife, Lisa. At one point he reported that the pilots were down, and one of the hijackers had a bomb strapped to himself. Sarah Bradshaw, a flight attendant, told her husband that she was getting ready to attack the hijackers with boiling hot water. At 9:55 the operator connected to Todd Beamer's cell phone heard him call out a charge—"Are you guys ready? Okay. Let's roll!"[2] The plane smashed into the peaceful Pennsylvania countryside eight minutes later, tragically killing everyone, but sparing more devastation to the nation's capital.

The North Tower of the World Trade Center buckled at 10:28.

A total of 2,998 people and nineteen hijackers died, with another 6,291 injured on that terrible day. In additional to the destruction of part of the Pentagon and the complete obliteration of the Twin Towers, many other buildings were either destroyed or badly damaged in the attacks.[3]

On Friday the 14th a service of prayer and remembrance took place at the National Cathedral in Washington. President Bush addressed the nation, often speaking in terms of the faith that incalculable numbers of Americans had held dear from the beginning of U.S. history:

> God's signs are not always the ones we look for. We learn in tragedy that his purposes are not always our own, yet the prayers of private suffering, whether in our homes or in this great cathedral are known and heard and understood.
>
> There are prayers that help us last through the day or endure the night. There are prayers of friends and strangers that give us strength for the journey, and there are prayers that yield our will to a will greater than our own.
>
> This world He created is of moral design. Grief and tragedy and hatred are only for a time. Goodness, remembrance and love have no end, and the Lord of life holds all who die and all who mourn.
>
> It is said that adversity introduces us to ourselves. This is true of a nation as well. In this trial, we have been reminded and the world has seen that our fellow Americans are generous and kind, resourceful and brave.
>
> We see our national character in rescuers working past exhaustion, in long lines of blood donors, in thousands of citizens who have asked to work and serve in any way possible. And we have seen our national character in eloquent acts of sacrifice. Inside the World Trade Center, one man who could have

saved himself stayed until the end and at the side of his quadriplegic friend. A beloved priest died giving the last rites to a firefighter. Two office workers, finding a disabled stranger, carried her down 68 floors to safety.

A group of men drove through the night from Dallas to Washington to bring skin grafts for burned victims. In these acts and many others, Americans showed a deep commitment to one another and in an abiding love for our country. . .

America is a nation full of good fortune, with so much to be grateful for, but we are not spared from suffering. In every generation, the world has produced enemies of human freedom. They have attacked America because we are freedom's home and defender, and the commitment of our fathers is now the calling of our time.

On this national day of prayer and remembrance, we ask almighty God to watch over our nation and grant us patience and resolve in all that is to come. We pray that He will comfort and console those who now walk in sorrow. We thank Him for each life we now must mourn, and the promise of a life to come.

As we've been assured, neither death nor life nor angels nor principalities, nor powers nor things present nor things to come nor height nor depth can separate us from God's love.

May He bless the souls of the departed. May He

comfort our own. And may He always guide our country.

God bless America.[4]

Todd Beamer's wife, Lisa, gave birth to their third child, Morgan, four months after the 9/11 attacks. A woman of abiding faith in Jesus Christ, she told *Decision* Magazine, "My relationship with God through Jesus has been the driving force in my life since my childhood, giving me hope for this life and for eternity." She said that it was just that expectation of the life to come that helped her cope since the loss of her young husband.

God has shown me the reality of eternity in a dynamic way these past few months. When I'm overwhelmed with sadness at what I've lost in this life, He is quick to give me His eternal perspective. "Lisa, this life is just a blip on the radar screen compared to your future with Me in heaven," He says. "The best thing that you can imagine on earth is garbage compared to what awaits you."[5]

END NOTES

1. "United Airlines Flight 93," Wikipedia Contributors, Wikipedia, *The Free Encyclopedia*, http://en.wikipedia.org/wiki/United_Airlines_Flight_93, October 20, 2008.

2. Ibid.

3. "September 11 Attacks," Wikipedia Contributors,

Wikipedia, *The Free Encyclopedia*, http://en.wikipedia.org/wiki/September_11_attacks#Damage, October 20, 2008.

4. Transcript of President Bush's Prayer Service Remarks, National Day of Prayers and Remembrance for the Victims of the Terrorist Attacks on September 11, 2001, Washington National Cathedral, September 14, 2001, U.S. Office of Personnel Management, http://www.opm.gov/guidance/09-14-01gwb.htm

5. "The Hope I Know," Lisa Beamer, *Decision*, September 2002, 8.

About the Author

Dr. Rebecca Price Janney is a theologically trained historian and author of sixteen books, including *Who Goes There? A Cultural History of Heaven and Hell, Great Women in American History, Great Stories in American History, Harriet Tubman,* and two young adult series as well as hundreds of articles in magazines and newspapers.

A graduate of Lafayette College and Princeton Seminary, Rebecca received her doctorate from Biblical Seminary. She resides with her husband and son in suburban Philadelphia